CENTRAL POWER IN THE
AUSTRALIAN COMMONWEALTH

Also by Sir Robert Menzies:

SPEECH IS OF TIME

VIRGINIA LEGAL STUDIES

Sponsored and supported by the School of Law of the University of Virginia for the publication of meritorious original works and reprints in law and related fields.

Central Power in the Australian Commonwealth

AN EXAMINATION
OF THE GROWTH
OF COMMONWEALTH POWER
IN THE
AUSTRALIAN FEDERATION

by

The Rt. Hon.
Gordon

Sir Robert Menzies

K.T., C.H., F.R.S., Q.C.

THE UNIVERSITY PRESS OF VIRGINIA,
CHARLOTTESVILLE

Library of Congress Catalog Card Number: 67-28061

Printed in Great Britain

FOR

OWEN DIXON

Contents

I am indebted to Professor Geoffrey Sawer, of the Australian National University, for some helpful suggestions in relation to my Lecture on the *Engineers' Case*; and to Dr. W. Anstey Wynes for his book to which I make reference. I also make a bow to Mr. Edgar Shannon, President of the University of Virginia, whose initiative made it possible for me to prepare and deliver these Lectures in Thomas Jefferson's great and famous University; Hardy Dillard, Dean of the Law Faculty at Virginia, whose friendship and encouragement did so much for me, and his colleagues, whom I liked so much; my good friend, Robert Harris, Dean of the Faculty of Arts and Sciences, and himself a notable constitutional lawyer; and George Spicer, of the same Faculty, who saved me from any temptation to be idle.

I do not mention by name the others who treated my wife and me with such warmth and generosity, but they will know.

I

Introduction

THESE studies represent an attempt on my part to analyse and explain a political and legal process of constitutional growth in the Australian Federation. I have seen this process from both sides, and have written with experience of both.

In my time as Prime Minister of Australia, I have had occasion to say to my United Kingdom political friends, rather less than half-jestingly, that though they or their predecessors had, in a legislative sense, created several Federations, two of which—Rhodesia and Nyasaland, and the West Indies—had already come apart, they had never been called upon to manage a Federation or experience its day to day problems.

Yet, in the English-speaking world which embraces three federal countries, the United States, Canada and Australia, it seems essential that both the principles of federalism and the nature of its internal stresses and strains should be understood and be studied, not just as a lawyer's exercise, but as something of very great practical political significance.

We have had, in Australia, a long series of valuable studies and expositions by constitutional lawyers, judicial, practising at the Bar, or academic. But I have long felt that there is room for some special examination of the interplay of law and political policy and developments in the Australian Federation.

Hence the theme I selected for my American lectures.

My treatment of the theme is, of course, limited and

therefore imperfect, but it may serve to stimulate more highly qualified and extensive studies than I could now hope to engage in.

Those who were, like me, brought up on the fundamental constitutional studies of A. V. Dicey and Lord Bryce will remember in particular the latter's exposition of the two forces which operate in a federation; the *centripetal* and the *centrifugal*. Expanding this, I believe that all modern experience has shown that in a federation, where powers are distributed between the National Government and State or provincial governments, there will develop either a movement, conscious or unconscious, to increase powers at the centre, or an opposite movement to increase the State or provincial powers at the expense of the central authority. In short, though the process may be a long one, federations tend either to become more dominated by the centre, with perhaps a perceptible public sentiment in favour of complete union, or to break up into their fractions. The latter process, for understandable local political and historical reasons, operated quite quickly in the two cases I referred to earlier. The former process is clearly visible in the United States and Australia, though in neither case is there any majority disposition to abandon federation for a closer form of organic union.

The two inevitable tendencies recorded by Bryce, and clearly visible in those federations which have endured, deserve consideration by those who look forward to some form of European federation.

True, I have several times had it put to me by British statesmen, who favour entry into the European Common Market, that they do not contemplate anything more than some form of limited *con*federation of European States; that they recognize that a federation would affect and materially modify the sovereignty of the constituent States, and that such a result would not be acceptable. But I know of nothing in constitutional history which would encourage the idea that *con*federations have permanency. They either come apart at the seams, or develop into federations with a closely defined organic structure.

I have elaborated these ideas in my first Virginian lecture.

It will be understood that, in what I have here written, I am not presuming to pronounce a judgment on what Great Britain should do about Europe; her people are eminently capable of deciding that for themselves. But I believe that there is something to be learned from the experience of others who have lived and worked in federations under what I will call 'constitutions in action'.

Broadly, what I set out to do in the lectures now embodied in this book, is to demonstrate how it has come about, in Australia, that the powers of the Central Government, though defined and therefore in form limited by a written Constitution, have tended to grow far beyond the conception of the original draftsmen; to some extent, it is true, as a result of formal amendment of the language of the Constitution itself, but to a material extent as a result of new and extended judicial interpretation of existing powers, with a marked tendency to aggregate financial power (and therefore political power) in the hands of the Parliament and Government of the nation.

I have not undertaken the very controversial political task of arguing whether this growth is good or bad. I am, particularly for a large continent with widely scattered communities, with great regional or local problems and understandable local prides and patriotisms, a Federalist. At our present stage of development, and for a long time to come, State Parliaments and Governments are and will be essential. The Constitution itself contemplates their continued existence and respects the powers 'reserved' to them.

But I cannot pretend that the growth of Commonwealth power which I have made it my task to describe does not present great problems of future adjustment for both Commonwealth and States if both are to co-exist and succeed.

In theory, some revised demarcation of powers could achieve this result; but, as the record of attempted amendments set out hereafter will show, the Australian electors (of whom I write with the respect due to people who accorded me their confidence for so many years!) have shown a marked reluctance to vote for constitutional amendments. Even those who feel that changes should be made, and they may well be in a majority, frequently develop uncertainties when the dry language of a proposed Amendment is submitted to them, and so, being in doubt, vote 'No', for reasons of prudence.

2

A General Consideration of the Theme, with reference to the Problems of Formal Constitutional Amendment

MR PRESIDENT, and Ladies and Gentlemen, it seems a very poor return for such an eloquent and flattering introduction to proceed to deliver what may turn out to be a prosaic lecture. In the Australian Parliament in which I lived and moved and had my being for thirty-one years, we had an engaging procedure which amounted to this: that an honourable member who claimed to have been misrepresented had the right to make a personal explanation. Now, I have not yet been misrepresented, though I have the shrewd idea I will be before the next three months are gone, but I will get in early and make my personal explanation ahead of any misrepresentation.

I think I ought to explain to you how I come to be here. Why should a man who sought relief from the labours and responsibilities of a Prime Minister accept the very considerable labour (although it is a great pleasure at the same time) of preparing and delivering *seven* lectures at the University of Virginia? Well, I will explain the mystery.

It has partly been unravelled for you tonight by the President. I came here in 1963 to deliver the Jefferson Memorial Speech. This was, of course, a tremendous honour, and I took it and understood it as such. But I really think that my greatest pleasure on that occasion, President, was not in making the speech, because, really, the pleasure of making a speech is easily overestimated. My greatest pleasure was to visit this quite lovely University. This University represents a combination, rare in this world, of vision and achievement by very great men, and the beauties which delighted my eyes on that occasion have now expanded, because I realize that I then saw only a fraction of it. The more I see of it, the more I love it. It is beyond question one of the most beautiful universities in the world. As we went around on that occasion, three years ago, your President talked, and I listened; he talked and I looked. And, influenced both by the ear and the eye, I found myself, I think it was after dinner, somewhat emotionally half-promising (that is all) to come here if and when I become relieved of office to give 'two or three' lectures on some comparative constitutional problem which might prove to be within my scope. Well, I recently retired from the Prime Ministership and from Parliament; still, I hope, though I have no reason to be dogmatic about the matter, *compos mentis*. I had almost forgotten my post-prandial half-promise. But your energetic and flattering President had not. Within forty-eight hours, I heard from him and before many more days had gone by, I had said 'yes'. And so here I am, Sir, my bluff called, to deliver *seven* lectures on what I have decided to call 'The growth of Commonwealth power in the Australian Federation.' I must say for the President that he stipulated only for six. But as I got to work I found, and this is not an uncommon experience for a politician, that it would take me seven lectures to say what I wanted to say. Now, Sir, let me say at once that I do not propose to do a general exercise in Australian constitutional law, in the provisions and interpretations of the Constitution of the Commonwealth of Australia. Legal scholars have written on these matters and I remind you that I am a scholar here only by courtesy. And those true scholars have sought to extract general rules from the judgments of the High Court of Australia and the Judicial Committee of the Privy Council, the judgments of the High Court being already enshrined in over one hundred tall volumes of the Commonwealth Law Reports.

Now, sir, my purpose is much more limited, but it may turn out (I hope it will) to be useful in a small way.

In this initial lecture, I want to define the nature of the task I have undertaken and to explain to you, if that turns out to be necessary, the nature and limitations of my qualifications to address you.

First of all the task. Had I been invited to make a technical, legal exposition of the Constitution of the Commonwealth of Australia—a body of study with which, in my days as a student and at the Bar, I was enthusiastically familiar—I would have been compelled to remember that it is eighteen long years since I stood up in Court, that I have not been able to keep up with the current of decision, and that I should decline the honour. True, in the past few months, sir, I have been 'revisiting the glimpses of the moon', and trying to bring myself up-to-date on the effect of that moon on the tides of judicial decision. But it is still true that I am not going to try to speak to you as a lawyer, in the well-known phrase, 'pure and simple'.

But it has been much in my mind that constitutional development is much more than a lawyer's exercise. It is the product of a fascinating mixture of legalism, politics, public psychology, sociology, whatever label you care to put on these exercises. In my own country, I could claim to know something about it. For the truth is that for many years I have been in the middle of a process which needs description, and the description of which may be of value to scholars both in your country and my own.

As a law student at the Melbourne University, I paid some special attention to the law of the Constitution. At the Bar, I appeared in many constitutional cases. My second lecture in this series will be about a case of the most far reaching consequences in which I had the impertinence to accept a brief at the age of twenty-five before the High Court of Australia. And if it is any encouragement to any of you, I won. Then, as you have been told, I went into State politics. I became Attorney-General of Victoria, and in that capacity I fought a few battles against what we regarded then as brutal Commonwealth encroachment on what we call 'State Rights'.

Well, sir, the times have changed, and no doubt I have changed with them, as will later appear. But I mention this autobiographical detail to show you that I have seen both sides of the case; the State side as well as the Federal. Then, I went into the Commonwealth Parliament. I was Attorney-General for five years; then I became Prime Minister. I was in office for two and a half years and was then found out and dismissed into outer darkness. And then I was in opposition for eight years, for six years of which I led a diminished Opposition, and then, by one of those tardy acts of justice which will occur even in politics, I became Prime Minister once more and remained there for sixteen or seventeen years until the only reasonable hope of getting out was to resign, which I did.

Now, of course, in that last period of years, a very formative period in Australian politics, I naturally had to preside over many conferences and engage in many discussions with State Premiers and with State Ministers.

I do not need to tell you in this country that the relations between the Central Government and the States are inevitably, in a federation, most complex. Developments occur every year, some of them almost invisible to the purely legal onlooker, but all of them clear and familiar to the men on the inside (or at least I like to think so).

It is because of this combination of legal and political experience in the constitutional field that I hope to be not altogether unqualified to address myself to the subject matters of these lectures.

Now in my years at the Bar, and in constitutional cases, I thought and spoke as a lawyer, viewing the structure of government from the outside, as it were. As a political minister, and particularly as a Prime Minister, I learned that things look different from the inside. This is what you might call the 'seamy side' of constitutionalism. But anyhow they do look different. One becomes conscious of the need for power if great policies are to be effective. One frequently chafes at the legalism of a federal system, though one knows that federalism is legalism. But one also discovers, as I have over the years, that in a federal system there may be shifts in power, alterations in the balance of power, which are quite independent of actual amendments to the constitutional document itself. There may also be new interpretations of old powers which would not have been anticipated by the draftsmen of our Constitution of 1900.

It is about such matters that I propose to speak to you during this term; not as a lawyer addressing his betters in the academic field, but as a lawyer-politician who had the chief responsibility for the National Government in its dealings with the States for almost thirty per cent of the life of the Commonwealth of Australia. In short, I want to speak within my own qualifications and experience, dealing with 'the Constitution in action' and some of the developments in practice which have occurred, and are still going on.

Now I am delighted to find that here in the United States Bryce's book on the American Commonwealth is still read. I am glad of that because I read it assiduously as a student myself. And you will remember that he had something to say about the movements that inevitably go on in a federal system; either the centripetal movements, leading of course to a growth of power at the centre, or the centrifugal movements, strengthening the States and 'State Rights' and leading to a corresponding weakening of central authority.

In your own history you have had much and sometimes

[9]

bitter experience of the conflict between these two forces. In Australia, we have fortunately escaped too sharp a conflict, though it is still fashionable in some quarters in Australia (and now I know I come on to delicate ground) to claim that the States are 'sovereign', and to treat the Commonwealth as if it were an outside power.

Bryce had some illuminating things to say about this— I quote with your permission (it is a passage that many of you will know very well).

> What State sovereignty means and includes was a question which incessantly engaged the most active legal and political minds of the nation, from 1789 right down to 1870. It is worth recalling that some thought that State sovereignty was paramount to the rights of the Union. Some, on the other hand, considered it as held in suspense by the Constitution, but capable of reviving [should there be secession from the Union]. Some maintained that each State had in accepting the Constitution finally renounced its sovereignty, which thereafter existed only in the sense of such an undefined domestic legislative and administrative authority as had not been conferred upon the Federal Congress.

It was, sir, among other things, if I may be so bold as to say it, the conflict between these views which helped to produce the Civil War. It is occasionally forgotten that the Civil War was not all about Uncle Tom's Cabin, although as a child in the bush in Australia I fervently believed that it was. Bryce went on to say: 'Since the defeat of the Secessionists, the last of these views may be deemed to have been established' and he adds with, to me, a wry touch of humour, 'the term "State sovereignty" is now but seldom heard'. He was, of course, not referring to Australia!

I will, sir, I assume, not need to remind you that your Federation and our own, although there are great differences in what I will call the 'machinery' of government, a matter that I might like to discuss at some stage when I am here, have certain broad elements in common; a central Government and as we say 'Parliament' exercising specific powers, and State Governments and 'Parliaments' exercising residuary powers over the same citizens regarded as either citizens of the nation or citizens of the individual State. You have a Supreme Court, as we have a High Court, to decide judicially the mutual limits of power and the validity of laws.

Each of our Constitutions has a demarcation of legislative powers, and a demarcation of legislative, executive and judicial functions.

In Australia, the relative positions of Commonwealth and States, and the interpretation and the demarcation of powers, have developed in a variety of ways. I will just briefly summarize them at this stage.

There has been development by formal amendment (a little); there has been development by new judicial rules of interpretation, or the new application of old ones; there has been development based upon the realization that well-known powers can be used for purposes never contemplated by the original draftsmen; and there has been development by those centripetal forces which, in any enduring federation, operate sometimes beneath the surface.

I will endeavour to deal with these in an orderly way. But, since the other elements are much less obvious to a distant observer than is the first—formal amendment—I will in this lecture seek to deal with the first, in order to clear the ground for the others.

FORMAL AMENDMENTS TO THE CONSTITUTION

You are, of course, all quite familiar with the provision in the United States Constitution for amendments to the Constitution. Briefly, the provision reads: 'The Congress, whenever two-thirds of both Houses shall deem it necessary,

[11]

shall propose amendments to this Constitution, or, on the application of the legislatures of two-thirds of the several States, shall call a convention for proposing amendments, which, in either case, shall be valid to all intents and purposes, as part of this Constitution, when ratified by the legislatures of three-fourths of the several States, or by conventions in three-fourths thereof, as the one or the other mode of ratification may be proposed by the Congress.' I omit the remainder of the provision as not material for my present purpose.

Well, in the case of the Australian Commonwealth Constitution, the provision for amendment is quite different. You will find it in Section 128 of the Commonwealth Constitution and it reads in this way (I will not read it all, but enough to make its point):

This Constitution shall not be altered except in the following manner:

The proposed law for the alteration thereof must be passed by an absolute majority of each House of the Parliament, and not less than two or more than six months after its passage through both Houses the proposed law shall be submitted in each State to the electors qualified to vote for the election of members of the House of Representatives.

But if either House passes any such proposed law by an absolute majority, and the other House rejects or fails to pass it or passes it with any amendment to which the first-mentioned House will not agree, and if after an interval of three months the first-mentioned House in the same or the next session again passes the proposed law by an absolute majority with or without any amendment which has been made or agreed to by the other House, and such other House rejects or fails to pass it or passes it with any amendment to which the first-mentioned House will not agree, the Governor-General may submit the proposed law as last proposed by the first-mentioned House, and either with or without any amendments subsequently agreed to by both Houses, to the electors in each State qualified to vote for the election of the House of Representatives.

When a proposed law is submitted to the electors the vote shall be taken in such manner as the Parliament prescribes.

And if in a majority of the States a majority of the electors voting approve the proposed law, and if a majority of all the electors voting also approve the proposed law, it shall be presented to the Governor-General for the Queen's assent.

To this, later on, has been added by Statute a pleasing idea and that is that the people who vote for the amendment in Parliament delegate somebody (in my time I was the body) to write out a case, not more than two thousand words, explaining why people ought to vote 'yes'. And on the other side, somebody is appointed to write out a case (same length) explaining why people should vote 'no'. And every elector, in the event of a constitutional referendum in Australia, gets a pamphlet containing both cases. We have had no research made to discover how many people read them. If the proposal has a majority in four States out of the six, and if a majority of all the electors voting approve of the proposed law, then it is presented to the Governor-General for the Queen's assent.

Well, sir, it is a little whimsical to recall that a year after the establishment of the Commonwealth, the Supreme Court of Victoria—(we must not get our courts too mixed up. Each state in Australia has a Supreme Court. That is why we call our top court for Australia the High Court. The High Court corresponds to your Supreme Court of

the United States)—offered the view that this section provided
a 'much easier' method of amending the Constitution than
that in the United States. Well, I take leave to doubt that
statement. All our experience is to the contrary. For you have,
in fact, achieved amendments to your Constitution. Some
of them, in broad and general terms like the Bill of Rights
and the Due Process Clause and so on, have produced a
great body of litigation. All general statements unfailingly
will. But our own experience in Australia has been that the
Commonwealth Constitution is susceptible to amendment
only with the greatest possible difficulty. I would just like to
tell you something (I hope not at tedious length) about the
attempts that have been made in the past. There was an
amendment, the very first amendment that was brought
forward, in 1906, and it was actually carried. There is a
landmark in Australian constitutional history! What was it?
Well, it dealt with the purely technical question of the rotation of Senators, and as the average person, I fear, does not
care how frequently a Senator rotates, the amendment was
carried. There was another amendment in 1910 relating to
payments to the States. It was defeated. But in the same year
another amendment was carried, for the very good reason
that it provided that the Commonwealth could take over
from the States their public debts. And this, as I do not need
to tell you, had an instant appeal in every State! It carried
easily.

In the following year, there was in office a government
that had high ambitions to increase the powers of the Commonwealth. It put forward proposals dealing with trade
and commerce, with corporations, with monopolies. (Monopolies used to be a wonderful slogan for many years. 'We
must have power to deal with monopolies.') These were all
rejected.

In 1913, a further proposal was put up for giving the
Commonwealth Parliament power over corporations. This

was defeated. In the same year, proposals in relation to power over labour, employment and unemployment were defeated; another proposal for power over monopolies was defeated; and a proposal that the Commonwealth power over conciliation and arbitration—a power to which I will have occasion to refer later on—should exist, validly, in relation to disputes, industrial disputes, in the railway service of a State, was defeated. In the same year, another proposal for extending the trade and commerce power was defeated. In the same year, another proposal to deal with trusts, combinations and monopolies was defeated. You can see that in this period of a a few years the then Commonwealth Government was very eager but uniformly unsuccessful, though it did in fact otherwise enjoy the confidence of the electors.

Now in 1919, after the First World War, there had been a considerable expansion of authority in the Commonwealth under the defence power. So proposals were put up once more in relation to trade and commerce, and 'corporations' and 'industrial matters' and the 'nationalization of monopolies'. They were all defeated.

In 1926, there was a tremendous amount of trouble on the waterfront. The Bruce Government put up a proposal to give the Commonwealth power to make laws 'protecting the interests of the public in case of actual or probable interruption of any essential service'. One would have expected this amendment to achieve a good deal of support at a time when there was widespread public dissatisfaction with the interruption of essential services. But the ingrained habit of voting 'no' prevailed.

In the same year they had another one on industry and commerce; it was thrown out. And then in 1928 I come to what I might call a 'break through' (forget about those little ones I mentioned earlier; they were of no moment). A proposal was put up, which is now Section 105A of the Commonwealth Constitution, on which I have prepared a lecture which will be delivered later on, relating to and validating a Financial Agreement that had been executed between the Commonwealth and the States. And that amendment was carried. Now on this occasion there was no great mystery about the reason. I remember it very well because I was a member of the Victorian Bar at that time, and with another lawyer, I was invited to advise the Premier of the State of Victoria about what was then the proposed Financial Agreement. The Premier of Victoria at that time was a gentleman named Hogan and he was a shrewd, earthy character. We as lawyers pointed out, and I think quite rightly, the disabilities that might arise from a State point of view if the agreement came into operation and was given constitutional authority and backing. But when the opinion was presented to the then Premier of Victoria, he read it through somewhat hastily, noticed that it was critical in its terms, but promptly said to the Crown solicitor: 'I'm not very much interested in this. If I sign this agreement, I'll get some Commonwealth money in my Budget next year.' That settled it. Every State thought that it saw some profit in the deal and this, of course, influenced the public, who are closer to State governments than they are to the National Government, and accordingly, the amendment was carried. That was the largest and most important amendment, as it turns out, ever made to the Commonwealth Constitution, and I will say more about it in a later lecture.

Well, then in 1937, when I was Attorney-General of the Commonwealth, we made a valiant but unsuccessful attempt to get the people of Australia to vote for an amendment to give control over civil aviation to the Commonwealth. Now, I would have thought that if ever there was a matter that called for national treatment rather than local, it was civil aviation. But it was defeated in no less than four States out of six. At the same time, we tried to secure an amendment to Section 92, the Interstate Free Trade provision, one of the glories of layman's language. 'Trade, commerce, and intercourse among the States shall be absolutely free.' A lovely expression! Nobody has yet quite certainly determined what it means. We wanted to change it because we wanted to have power to limit the operation of Section 92 so as to validate the organized marketing of goods, particularly primary products. That proposal arose from the fact that the Privy Council had invalidated Commonwealth marketing legislation in spite of a powerful and persuasive argument by myself before their Lordships' Board. Our proposal was defeated by almost a million votes in a total poll of three and three quarter millions, and it was defeated in all six States. And what is more, at the succeeding General Election, my constituents in the electorate of Kooyong, which is, as you may suppose, an eminently respectable electorate, who normally returned me with majorities of fifteen thousand, almost voted me out. They did not like my referendum, and I won by fifteen hundred, not fifteen thousand. Now I think all that will confirm the view that I am putting to you, that constitutional amendments in Australia are not easy.

Well, the story does not end there. I will hasten on with it. In 1944, the then Labour Government put forward fourteen proposals; they made a very great tactical error (as my political opponents occasionally did). They put them all in one Bill—a mixed grill, as you might say, of new powers— which therefore required one vote, so that if anybody was opposed to any one of the fourteen he would vote 'no' to the lot. Well, most people did, and the proposals were rejected in four States out of six.

Then in 1946, the High Court of Australia gave a decision which cast more than grave doubt on the validity of certain social services that had been introduced and, in consequence, an amendment was put forward to clarify the Commonwealth's power in relation to those matters.

It was almost unopposed in Parliament—I think I remember correctly that only one Member in either House voted against it (and he was one of those chaps who would have voted against himself if it came to the pinch)—so that here was all-Party support for a proposal which touched and concerned almost every individual in Australia. It was carried; but it was carried by only three hundred and seventy thousand votes in a total poll of four and a quarter millions! At the same time then, the same Government tried to secure power over marketing, and it lost.

Then they had another go in the same year about industrial employment, and that was defeated. Then they, in 1948, put up a proposal to give the Commonwealth power over 'rents and prices'. Now you would have thought, would you not, though I personally opposed the Bill for a variety of reasons, that this would have proved to be rather popular in the immediate post-war period when both 'rents and prices' tended to rise. Yet, the proposal to give this power to the Commonwealth was easily defeated in all States.

And finally, in 1951, my own Government put up a proposal that the Commonwealth should have power to deal with Communists and Communism. The proposal was defeated, by fifty-two thousand in a poll of four and three quarter millions. It was carried in three States, but it was defeated in three, and therefore it failed to secure approval under Section 128.

It may interest you, and I say this at the risk of protracting this lecture too long, to hear some special comment on this episode.

The failure of that Communist referendum campaign was, I have thought, influenced, though perhaps not primarily, by the Australian public acceptance of the High Court of Australia as essentially a non-political body. This is something important to remember, when you consider these matters. For a reason which seemed to us in the Government to be compelling, we had drafted our constitutional amendment in two parts. The first part was as follows:

1. The Constitution is altered by inserting after Section 51 the following Section:

51 A(1) The Parliament shall have power to make such laws for the peace, order and good government of the Commonwealth with respect to Communists or Communism as the Parliament considers to be necessary or expedient for the defence or security of the Commonwealth or for the execution or maintenance of this Constitution or of the laws of the Commonwealth.

Now there was, and is, in Australia a very strong and indeed overwhelming opposition to Communism. If our proposed amendment had ended there, I think it would have been carried. But would it have been sufficient for the purpose? Rightly or wrongly, we thought not. The Communist Party Dissolution Act of the previous year, to which I will make fuller reference when I come to examine the defence powers in a later lecture, had sought to pursue Communist bodies in their different forms and under different names because Communism has an elusive quality. It had for example, in the Bill, given power to the Governor-General, i.e., to the Executive Council made up of Ministers, to declare certain bodies of persons in effect Communist, to be unlawful. Then, any such body could apply to the Court to set aside the declaration.

It was objected that this placed the onus on the declared body; and this argument was, as you might suppose, readily made popular by those who advocated 'civil liberties'. This placed the Government on the horns of a dilemma. Governments are always on the horns of a dilemma. Should we have a statutory form which, at all stages, put on to the Commonwealth the onus of proving Communist beliefs or associations; an onus which very frequently could not be discharged without exposing in Court, and to the Communists, the personnel and apparatus of the Security Intelligence Organization? Or should we proceed by declaration, with power to apply to the contrary?

Rightly or wrongly, we chose the latter course, to avoid securing a power which might turn out to be ineffective.

And, therefore, the second part of our proposed constitutional amendment asked people to approve, in particular, of giving the Commonwealth power to make a law in terms of the Communist Party Dissolution Act of 1950.

Well, as the referendum campaign went on, the debate, I would not need to tell you, raged less and less about outlawing the Communists, and more and more about the contentious details of the Act. And in the end, as I have pointed out, a strongly anti-Communist electorate failed to give us a majority. This means that the Commonwealth Parliament has no power to deal directly with the Communist Party or with Communism and its subsidiaries as such, and is left with the normal provisions of the Commonwealth Crimes Act relating to treason, and sedition, and advocacy of the overthrow of the Constitution by violence and so on.

The whole matter afforded interesting evidence that the electors, when they have the chance, are not only reluctant to vote for new powers for the Commonwealth but are also, by deep instinct, unwilling to modify in any way the old principle that 'a man is innocent until he is *proved* guilty'.

You will see from this brief historical narrative that so far from being easily amendable the Commonwealth Constitution of Australia will be amended only with great difficulty and under very special circumstances.

Well, you may ask, as we have asked ourselves, why is this so. Could I just offer you as briefly as possible a reason or two. First of all, an amendment of the Constitution has to be put in statutory form. Remember, if you may, the words that I was referring to earlier, 'the proposed *law* shall be submitted to the people'. And when even the simplest proposal is put into statutory form, in a Bill, which has to pass both Houses before being put to the people, it assumes a technical appearance, which induces in the lay mind a deep suspicion and distrust. The layman is very readily left in doubt, and when in doubt he votes 'No'.

As I pointed out some years ago to a University audience in Australia (do you mind if I just quote myself very briefly?):

> Constitutional problems attract little public attention except during the actual currency of a campaign; and even then there tends to be rather more heat than light. This is not surprising. Federalism is in its very nature legalistic. A proper understanding of it involves a considerable intellectual exercise in both synthesis and analysis. The very notion of Federal and State Governments elected by and dealing with the same people, but with sovereign powers divided between them according to the terms of a legal instrument as interpreted from time to time by the judiciary, is a very complex notion. Many try to understand it, and confess failure. Many, perhaps wisely, do not even try. This is basically the reason why constitutional amendment by popular vote has proved so difficult.

Again, sir, there is in my country, normally, a considerable distrust of or hostility to central authority. It is a curious thing, but States which have bemused themselves, as they very frequently have, by what I call the fallacy of the 'sovereign' State, readily fall into the error of thinking the Commonwealth is a foreign power, and that you must not give it too much authority. You must clip its wings. And therefore any proposal to increase the power of the Commonwealth, unless there are compensating factors for the States, has, normally, a very slim chance of being carried. There is something rather ironical about this, because the practice has arisen in every State in Australia, I would think, of taking all problems of the provision of funds to Canberra. I suppose you know nothing of this in the United States, but it is quite common in Australia. It is so easily said about any local problem, 'Well, why don't you take this to Canberra? Why don't you get the Commonwealth to do something about it?' And yet, while this goes on, paradoxically enough, the very people who are saying, why doesn't the Commonwealth do something about it, go to great pains to see that the Commonwealth has no power to do something about it.

Well, these may or may not be the exact reasons. Behind them all is the historic fact that federation came about in Australia, not primarily by the presence of a common danger or external threat, but by a process of domestic argument which extended over many years, involved several conventions which engaged the labours of some of the best minds in the country, and led to two referendums in 1898 and 1899 before general approval had been secured and the Constitution could be presented to the British Parliament for enactment.

Now, through all that period, there were the great enthusiasts like Edmund Barton and Alfred Deakin in Australia who, in eloquent terms, envisaged a new nation; 'one land, one flag, one destiny'. You can imagine it all. But there were many who distrusted the venture. If I were asked to select the most remarkable feature of the creation of our Commonwealth I would say this, that speaking broadly, *we federated with a great deal of reluctance; in other words, the disjunctive forces, the centrifugal forces, were in fact at their strongest just before the argument about federation began.* They had to be broken down before people could be induced to come together. It is quite true that we had in Australia very many of the elements that have usually made for unity in the political history of the world: community of race, a common language (which, subject to some modifications, we share with you), common traditions, common institutions; to a very large extent we had

[22]

a common religion, and we had common sports and games. Now all these matters are those which will normally drive people into unity, and one would have expected that federation would have been a matter of rapid consummation. *But there stood in the way of federation at least two very powerful factors*; one, the desire of each State to have its own fiscal policy (Victoria, for example, was a protectionist colony and New South Wales was a free trade colony; and they wanted each of them to have its own fiscal policy), and the second, of course, was the natural insistence by small communities on their own rights and indeed their own virtues.

The matter was very well put by my own old law professor, Sir Harrison Moore, in these words: 'The absence of urgent external affairs in Australian politics favoured the growth of that rivalry and bitterness which is common in small contiguous communities.' And I may add that anybody who travels from State to State in Australia will agree with me that the rivalry has by no means died away with sixty-five years of federation.

But that there should be resistance to the new move, and much jealousy and apprehension, was no doubt inevitable. You will be amused to know I think, well, I hope so, that one matter which at first induced New South Wales to oppose federation (you will find it hard to believe this although some of you have read it already), was that of the location of the Federal Capital. Sydney was afraid of domination by Melbourne should Melbourne become the Capital. Quite right; I am a Melbourne man myself. Melbourne reciprocated the fears. A compromise was arrived at and this persuaded New South Wales to vote 'yes' for the federation. This compromise is now Section 125: 'The seat of Government of the Commonwealth shall be determined by the Parliament, and shall be within territory which shall have been granted to or acquired by the Commonwealth, and shall be vested in and belong to the Commonwealth, and shall be in the

State of New South Wales, and be distant not less than one hundred miles from Sydney. . . .' And then it went on, 'The Parliament shall sit at Melbourne until it meets at the Seat of Government'.

Well, good came of it all, for, years afterwards, Canberra was chosen and established, and is rapidly, as I believe, becoming a thing of beauty and a focus of national pride.

I hope you will permit me, sir, before I conclude, one fairly cynical aside. One of the fears about Melbourne was that Members of the Parliament would be unduly influenced by the Melbourne Press, which would be available every morning. Nowadays, at Canberra, Members are to be seen every morning reading the newspapers of practically every capital city and, I suspect, being influenced by the lot!

The emotions and prejudices of the nineties have not entirely died away. They still have their influence on the fate of constitutional amendments.

But, as I will point out later on in my series, there are more ways than one of achieving constitutional development in a Federation.

Now, I am a Federalist myself. I believe as I am sure most of you do, that in the division of power, in the demarcation of powers between a Central Government and the State governments, there resides one of the true protections of individual freedom. And yet how true it is that as the world grows, as the world becomes more complex, as international affairs engage our attention more and more, and affect our lives more and more, it is frequently ludicrous that the National Parliament, the National Government, should be without power to do things which are really needed for the national security and advancement.

Now I will come back in a later lecture to the Financial Agreement, because I propose to indicate to you that although, with that exception, the amendments to the Commonwealth Constitution of Australia have been of relatively minor moment, there have been in fact tremendous changes in the balance of power, tremendous changes in practice, some of them as I indicated earlier arising from undercurrents, some of them due to unexpected results of new powers, some of them due to new interpretations, wider interpretations of Commonwealth powers, interpretations probably not originally contemplated. These things have gone on, and they have now become part of the fundamental law of Australia. I will deal with all those matters, sir, in their sequence. But, ladies and gentlemen, you will be much relieved to know, not tonight.

3

Growth by Judicial Interpretation of Commonwealth Powers
The Engineers' Case

Tonight, I must come to the fascinating problem of how a constitution develops by judicial interpretation. And the first question therefore is:

How should we interpret a Constitution, which is after all not a detailed Statute, but a frame of government? Should we interpret it as if it were an ordinary Act of Congress or of Parliament—that is to say, narrowly and literally, as if it were a Police Offences Act? I do not think that anybody nowadays would support this idea of constitutional interpretation. Indeed, if the High Court of Australia had supported it, the meaning attached and the operation given to the Commonwealth defence power, which will be the subject of my next lecture, in case any of you happen to be here, or the postal and telegraphic power, would have been very different from what has in fact been the case. I will deal with those examples at a later stage, but not tonight. But in the meantime, I simply say that the course of being narrow and literal and restrictive, must, you will agree, be rejected.

Well, there is a second possible way of interpreting the Constitution. Should we interpret the words loosely and politically, that is to say responding to the varying currents of political opinion? If so, interpretations will tend to fluctuate according to the political complexion of the judges. Now, having regard to Australian tradition, and it is of that

I am speaking tonight, I must reject this notion. I agree with something I will quote from Mr Justice Dixon, our most celebrated judicial lawyer, that 'federalism is legalism of necessity'. The Constitution must have an authority of its own. Dixon, in his speech to the Bar on his appointment to the Chief Justiceship in 1952, said these words, and they are worth recounting: 'Federalism means a demarcation of powers, and this casts upon the Court a responsibility of deciding whether legislation is within the boundaries of allotted powers. Unfortunately that responsibility is very widely misunderstood, misunderstood, largely, by the popular use and misuse of terms which are not applicable, and it is not sufficiently recognized that the Court's sole function is to interpret a constitutional description of power or restraint upon power and say whether a given measure falls on one side of a line consequently drawn or on the other, and that it has nothing whatever to do with the merits or demerits of the measure. Such a function has led us all I think to believe that close adherence to legal reasoning is the only way to maintain confidence of all parties in federal conflicts. It may be that the Court is thought to be excessively legalistic. I should be sorry to think that it is anything else. There is no other safe guide to judicial decisions in great conflicts than a strict and complete legalism.'

Now, I just want to pause to point out that when he used the expression 'excessively', I am sure he was using it in the sense in which it was used a great deal in the eighteenth and nineteenth centuries. I am 'excessively' happy to see you. It did not mean 'I am excessively happy beyond the bounds of propriety', but very pleased—very. So, substitute 'very', very legalistic.

Now, sir, ladies and gentlemen, if you are, as students of constitutions, repelled by the words 'complete legalism', I must point out to you one of the modern characteristics of the High Court of Australia was succinctly and, I think most accurately described by Professor Geoffrey Sawer, of the Australian National University, in a lecture he gave to the Emory University in Georgia, in 1958. He used these words:

> The appointment of Sir Owen Dixon as Chief Justice in 1952 [an appointment for which, I am proud to say, I was myself responsible] emphasized the dominance of the 'non-political' trend; Dixon is the greatest exponent of the analytic and conceptual type of English common-law thinking in Australian legal history, and probably the greatest living judge in that tradition in any English-speaking country. Of the men now on the Bench, only one has been associated with active politics; several have performed administrative tasks for Government, especially in wartime, but they are above all technical lawyers steeped in the professional tradition of the country and without experience in discharging the political responsibilities of government. The average age of the present seven at writing was only sixty-three; hence the present professional atmosphere of the Court, and the emphasis on a constitutional law of analytic concepts, may last for many years.

Having already, for myself, rejected the too narrow, and the too wide and fluctuating, I come down to the third possible course, that the interpretation ought to be sound in legal principle but flexible in application. A Constitution is designed to endure; it is not a temporary Statute. As a continuing document, it is designed to apply to changing circumstances, to new people, and to new modes of thought. In short, a Constitution is not a strait-jacket; it is a frame of government. To adopt the metaphor of Chief Justice Marshall in *McCulloch and Maryland* (4 Wheaton, 316), flesh must be put on the dry bones. The purpose of a Constitution is to authorize and facilitate action within ascertainable limits. Sir Isaac Isaacs, who at a later stage was Chief Justice of Australia, a prominent exponent of the 'progressive' school of interpretation, put it in this way in the case of the *Commonwealth* v. *the Colonial Combing Company* (1922, 31 C.L.R. at 438–9):

> It is the duty of the Judiciary to recognize the development of the nation and to apply established principles to the new positions which the nation in its progress from time to time assumes. The judicial organ would otherwise separate itself from the progressive life of the community, and act as a clog upon the legislative and executive departments rather than as an interpreter.

I merely pause to observe that there is in these words no such conflict with Mr Justice Dixon's 'legalism' as might appear. The emphasis is on the words 'established principles' (which must be of law) and 'an interpreter' (not a legislator).

So that you may have a proper basis for comparison with your own rules of judicial interpretation, I should point out that there is one very big difference between the constitutional problems which usually come before the High Court of Australia and those which usually come before the Supreme Court of the United States of America. Most cases in Australia concern the demarcation of powers as between the Commonwealth and the States. Our Constitution does not contain the kind of fundamental guarantee of individual rights—the 'Bill of Rights'—which your Constitution embodies. I am under the impression, I may be wrong, that most recent major constitutional cases in your Supreme Court arise in respect of the fundamental guarantees, which affect all governments, and not in relation to the demarcation of powers as between governments.

Now our demarcation problem in Australia no doubt lends itself more readily to handling along lines of established principles, with enduring though flexible concepts, than do problems of due process, equal protection, and the like. In the determination of your problems, it may be that there is more room for the political philosophy of the judge; I do not know. But I do know that in the determination of our type of problem the High Court has developed politically neutral conceptions of constitutional law; an honourable fact which occasionally brought defeat and anguish to my own Government! I say that, because, being politically neutral, though most of the judges had been appointed by my Government, they threw out incontinently some rather important legislation which we had promoted.

Now, that being established, we come to another question of interpretation—one which was hard-fought for years in Australia, and which I will deal with when I come to discuss what is in Australia the celebrated case—the *Engineers' Case*. Are the States, as organisms, to any and if so what extent, excluded from Commonwealth power? In the Australian Constitution, as in yours, specific powers are granted to the Commonwealth, the residue being left with the States.

It will, I think, appear that, a residual power being what is left after a specific power is taken out, it is only when you interpret the grant of the power to the Commonwealth, to the Central Government, and look at the express terms of the Commonwealth Constitution, that you can begin to consider what is the 'residue' left to the States. As one of our judges put it in a very homely but well-known way, 'the tail is not to wag the dog'.

Now, sir, this brings me to the story and significance of the *Engineers' Case* (1920. 28 C.L.R. 129).

This notable case, a landmark in Australian constitutional interpretation, deserves my rather careful exposition. There are two reasons for this. One is very important. It is that it represented a major constitutional development of Australian power, by disposing of earlier restrictive interpretations which had the effect of creating areas of implied immunity for State Governments and State instrumentalities.

The second reason is unimportant, but human. I was the sole counsel for the successful party. I was very young, twenty-five years old, and a success meant a great deal to me. In fact, I got married on the strength of it.

To appreciate the significance of the case, it is necessary to refer to the constitutional power involved. It was this [Section 51 (XXXV)]:

> The Parliament shall, subject to this Constitution, have power to make laws for the peace, order and good government of the Commonwealth with respect to conciliation and arbitration for the prevention and settlement of industrial disputes extending beyond the limits of any one state.

This was and is a very limited industrial power, the chief limitations being the confining of the means to 'conciliation' and 'arbitration', the limitations involved in the word 'industrial', since there had to be industrial disputes, and the requirement that they had to be interstate disputes. So you have these three sharply limiting factors.

Each of these expressions has been fruitful of litigation. I look back on it with a certain amount of gratitude because I was engaged in a good deal of it myself. But I will refrain from irrelevant reminiscence.

In the *Engineers' Case*, the President of the Commonwealth Court of Conciliation and Arbitration, the late Mr Justice Higgins (who was also a Justice of the High Court), stated a case which asked the High Court to decide whether the Commonwealth Court of Conciliation and Arbitration had power to make an award binding upon the State Implement and Engineering Works and the State Sawmills established by the Government of Western Australia, the relevant facts relating to which he set out in these terms.

The State Implement and Engineering Works and the State Sawmills were established by the Government of Western Australia, and are regulated by the relevant Acts of that Parliament.

The State Implement and Engineering Works undertake for the public as well as for the various State Departments the work of making and repairing agricultural implements, and engines, troughs, windmills, etc. They also undertake for private steamship owners, as well as for steamers owned by the State, repairs to ships and to shipping machinery.

They advertise their operations in competition with private undertakings in newspapers and by circulars, have show-rooms in Perth, and have selling agents throughout the State.

The State Sawmills cut and mill timber, and sell the product in competition with other mill-owners to the public, and carry out saw-mill works for the public as well as for the State Departments.

Now, sir, to understand the nature of the legal problem so presented, it is necessary to make some reference to the state of the High Court decisions as they stood at that time, in 1920.

The Court had, in its very first year, decided the case of *D'Emden* v. *Pedder* (1904. 1 C.L.R. 91). It held that a State could not tax a federal officer in respect of his federal salary, as such a tax would operate as an interference with the free exercise of the powers of the Commonwealth. It based its decision very naturally upon the famous judgment of Chief Justice Marshall in *McCulloch* v. *Maryland* (1819. 4 Wheaton 316), in which the Chief Justice stated, and you all are familiar with these words, his conviction 'that the States have no power, by taxation or otherwise, to retard, impede, burden, or in any manner control, the operation of the constitutional laws enacted by Congress to carry into execution the powers vested in the general government'. 'This is, we think', said Marshall, 'the unavoidable consequence of that supremacy which the Constitution has declared.'

The High Court of Australia declared the rule in its own words as follows:

> When a State attempts to give its legislative or executive authority an operation which, if valid, would fetter, control, or interfere with the free exercise of the legislative or executive power of the Commonwealth, the attempt, *unless expressly authorized by the Constitution*, is to that extent invalid and inoperative.

Now, each of these declarations always seemed to me to be clear, to be based on the interpretation of the powers specifically conferred on the central legislature, and to be based, and I again quote Marshall's famous words, 'on that *supremacy* which the Constitution has declared', and *not* designed, I would have thought, to have any reciprocal operation. Yet, before long the High Court of Australia, following, I am bound to tell you with all frankness, some decisions of the Supreme Court of the United States of America, which I suppose in its own time might have gone wrong, began to evolve principles of reciprocity.

I am not going to weary you with a wilderness of single instances, but I will give you two to illustrate this.

In 1906, only two years after *D'Emden and Pedder*, in the *Railway Servants' Case* (1906. 4 C.L.R. 488), the High Court of Australia held (and you will understand, ladies and gentlemen, that the High Court corresponds to your Supreme Court of the United States) that railways were, in Australia, government instrumentalities, their control and working being, as a matter of history in 1900, and as a matter of constitutional reference regarded as a function of government.

Now at that point, there was much to be said for this,

because our Constitution specifically provided, in several places, about railways.*

Therefore, there was something to be said for the idea that railways, being in effect, as to 99 per cent state activities in Australia, stood outside the Commonwealth power except for those purposes. Now, I ought to point out to you, because otherwise it might be confusing, that Australian railways, unlike yours, have for the most part been built and run by Governments. This has not been the result of some socialist theory; it is a heritage of nineteenth-century conditions. With a small and scattered population, national development required the construction of many non-paying railway lines to open up new country. And so governments took over and have for most of the time conducted their railways at a loss, for the public gain.

In the *Railway Servants' Case*, the High Court held that the rule in *D'Emden* v. *Pedder* operated both ways, and that the Commonwealth conciliation and arbitration power did not extend to enable industrial awards to be made against the States in right of their railways.

Now, sir, I would have thought that the doctrine laid down in *D'Emden and Pedder* was one based upon a full upholding of Commonwealth power unless, to quote the words I mentioned, the suggested limitation was 'expressly authorized by the Constitution'. Yet Chief Justice Griffith, speaking for the Court, having quoted the very words of *D'Emden and Pedder* and of *McCulloch and Maryland*, went on to say: 'In that case, the question was as to an attempted invasion of the ambit of Commonwealth authority by a

---

* Section 51 (xxxii) The control of railways with respect to transport for the naval and military purposes of the Commonwealth.

(xxxiii) The acquisition, with the consent of a State, of any railways of the State on terms arranged between the Commonwealth and the State.

(xxxiv) Railway construction and extension in any State with the consent of that State.

[34]

State authority. *The present case is the converse, but the doctrine is equally applicable.*'

This, to me, puzzling piece of reasoning was justified by reference to an American decision, with which no doubt many of you have been familiar, *Collector and Day* (11 Wallace 113), where the Supreme Court of the United States, through Mr Justice Nelson, said:

> In this respect, that is, in respect of the reserved powers, the State is as sovereign and independent as the general Government. And if the means and instrumentalities employed by that Government (the State Government) to carry into operation the powers granted to it are, necessarily, and, for the sake of self preservation, exempt from taxation from the States, why are not those of the States depending upon their reserved powers, for like reasons, equally exempt from federal taxation? Their unimpaired existence in the one case is as essential as in the other.

Well, I imagine, sir, that *Collector and Day* has, nowadays, what shall I say, a reduced reach in your constitutional law.

Refinements were of course introduced by the Courts of both countries. This is a phenomenon with which you are familiar, for whatever the doctrine, there must be limits somewhere. What State authorities or instrumentalities were exempted from Commonwealth or Federal action? Now it would be difficult to say that *all* were; for this would open the door for any State to take itself out of Commonwealth jurisdiction altogether by increasing the organic area of State action. A strongly Socialist State government could do this on the grand scale. Having regard to this obvious difficulty, a distinction came to be made, as you know, between what were somewhat euphemistically called 'the primary and inalienable functions of a constitutional government' (*Coomber and the Justices of Berkshire*) (9 App. Cas. 74) which would be protected, and the 'trading' activities of a State, which would not be protected.

Now the last case to give support to this distinction was decided only a year before the *Engineers' Case*.

It was the *Amalgamated Workers Union* v. *the Adelaide Milling Company* (1919. 26 C.L.R. 460). In that case it was held that States which were carrying on buying and selling operations, pursuant to an agreement with the Commonwealth for concerted action owing to the scarcity of means of transportation occasioned by the first Great War, were carrying on governmental, and not trading, activities, and stood outside the Commonwealth industrial power. It was thus made to appear that a wheat lumper so employed was unconsciously, but splendidly, performing one of the primary functions of government.

Barton, J., Mr Justice Barton, who had been the first Prime Minister of Australia, and was a Justice of the First High Court, expressing the doctrine which had been evolved by the Court, of which he was a distinguished member, said this. Remember that this was only a year before the *Engineers' Case*. He said:

> The case of *D'Emden* v. *Pedder* has become a settled authority and this Court only in September last intimated in Full Bench that the majority of the Justices were of opinion that it would be a waste of time to attack the decision of this Court in the *Railway Servants' Case*. In the last-named case the Court unanimously decided that the rule laid down in *D'Emden* v. *Pedder* was reciprocal. . . .

Mr Justice Isaacs, who had been critical of the reciprocal application of the rule in *D'Emden and Pedder*, agreed with the decision for reasons which reflected his overwhelming sense of the gravity of the war problem and his predisposition to give the defence powers a far-reaching and almost unlimited interpretation. He said:

Now, in this case, the whole scheme is dominated by the ultimate purpose, namely, the defence of the Empire. It must be steadily borne in mind that the acts dealt with in this case are all assumed to be lawful acts, and strictly within the legal powers of the Government concerned. And these legal acts were all aimed at the satisfaction of private needs, but for the one great public purpose. The character of trading being absent and the nature of the power being governmental, each of the questions put should be answered in the negative.

Well, sir, this was, from my point of view, the discouraging state of the decisions when, in 1920, I stood up before the Full High Court at Melbourne as counsel for the Union, the Amalgamated Society of Engineers, to argue that the Western Australian Government bodies were not immune from the Commonwealth conciliation and arbitration powers. Naturally, I began to argue that their functions were those of trading and not of government; as the decisions stood, no other line of argument seemed open. What is more, the respondents were clearly in their very description engaged in trading operations. Their Act of Parliament said so. The *Railway Servants' Case* could in reality be in my favour, since the basis of immunity in that case was that railways were functions of State Governments before Federation, and were therefore government instrumentalities under the then accepted doctrine of the 'immunity of instrumentalities'.

The application of the reasoning in that case would of course give no immunity in the West Australian case, because in the latter case there were trading functions created only within the last few years.

But in spite of some possibilities to the contrary, I felt pretty confident that, to decide the *Engineers' Case* in my favour, the Court would not be compelled to overrule the earlier decisions. But what happened was this. I was young, like you, ardent like some of you, fresh from a somewhat critical study of the Doctrine of Instrumentalities in my University days, and not unwilling to do a little tilting if the chance offered itself. Hence the somewhat brash remark which, in a moment, I will report. In addition, young as I was, I knew enough of the earlier dissenting opinions to hope that the Court, from which the earlier majority Justices had by this time disappeared, might be willing to seize upon the opportunity to re-open the whole matter, overruling the *Railway Servant's Case* in the process.

Well, what happened was that an hour or so after I had begun by developing this argument, distinguishing the *Railway Servants' Case*, doing lip service to the Doctrine, Mr Justice Starke, who was a very distinguished Common lawyer, and whose blunt habits of expression made no exception in favour of a very young man, looking at me in a grumbling way, said, 'This argument is a lot of nonsense!' [Now by courtesy of your distinguished librarian, I had a look this afternoon at something of the life of the famous American and English lawyer Benjamin, and I was fascinated to find that one of the English judges had said that to him once. He said, 'It's nonsense'. Yes! And with sturdy American independence, he was then at the English bar, he took great exception to this, folded up his papers and walked out of Court. Now, I did not know about that; anyhow, nothing could have persuaded me to walk out of Court. This was my first big brief in the High Court of Australia; I was not going to leave it.] So, when Starke said 'This argument is a lot of nonsense', I, in what I later realized to be an inspired moment, replied: 'Sir, I quite agree.' 'Well', intervened the Chief Justice, Chief Justice Knox, never the most genial of interrogators, 'why are you putting an argument which you admit is nonsense?' 'Because', said the young Menzies (the old Menzies would not have dared to do this) 'I am compelled by the earlier decisions of this

Court. If your Honours will permit me to question all or any of these earlier decisions, I will undertake to advance a sensible argument.' I waited for the heavens to fall. Instead, the Chief Justice said: 'The Court will retire for a few minutes.' And when they came back, he said, 'This case will be adjourned for argument at Sydney. Each government will be notified so that it may apply to intervene. Counsel will be at liberty to challenge any earlier decision of this Court!'

So, as they say in the love stories, that's how it all began. In Sydney, with a thickly populated, and from my lonely point of view, hostile Bar table, the essence of my argument, as summarized in the Law Reports was that 'the specific grant of power must be defined before the residue can be defined. The express grant is only to be cut down by express limitations. The maxim *Quando lex aliquid concedit* can only apply to a grant of power, and has no application to the powers of the States remaining after the federal powers have been taken out. For the purposes of this case, the word 'industrial' in Sub-Section 35, provides the only limitation. What is industrial if done by a private employer is industrial if done by a State.'

Well, when the judgment came to be delivered, it proved to be a great landmark in the history of interpretation. The Court did overrule the earlier decisions, and, because the judgment gave a new and what one legal authority had called an 'extensive' interpretation of Commonwealth powers, it is a great landmark in Australian constitutional development, and in the development of Commonwealth power.

The great majority of the judges made very short work, I am happy to say, of the proposition that the rule in *D'Emden and Pedder*, professing to affirm the rule in *McCulloch and Maryland*, had a reciprocal application in favour of the States. What they said was this:

It is said that the rule above stated must be read as

reciprocal, because some of the reasoning in *D'Emden and Pedder* indicates a reciprocal invalidity of Commonwealth law where the State is concerned. It is somewhat difficult to extract such a statement from the judgment; it would be *obiter* if found. It is said, however, that the later cases regard *D'Emden and Pedder* as supporting that view, and ultimately the doctrine of mutual non-interference finds its most distinct formulation in another case of the *Attorney-General for Queensland* v. *the Attorney-General for the Commonwealth* (20 C.L.R. 163). There, Chief Justice Griffith, assuming the implication of non-interference to arise prima facie from necessity in *all cases*, and then to be subject to *exclusion* where the necessity ended, proceeded to say: 'It is manifest that, since the rule is founded upon the necessity of the implication, the implication is excluded if it appears upon consideration of the whole Constitution that the Commonwealth, or conversely, the State, was intended to have power to do the act the validity of which is impeached.' 'Then', the *Engineers' Case* majority went on, 'how is that intention to be ascertained? The learned Chief Justice proceeds to ascertain it by reference to outside circumstances, not of law or constitutional practice, but of fact. . . . It is an interpretation of the Constitution depending on an implication which is formed on a vague, individual conception of the spirit of the compact, which is not the result of interpreting any specific language to be quoted, nor referable to any recognized principle of the common law of the Constitution, and which, when started, is rebuttable by an intention of exclusion equally not referable to any language of the instrument or acknowledged common law constitutional principle, but arrived at by the Court on the opinions of Judges as to hopes and expectations respecting vague external conditions.' 'This method of interpretation', they said, 'cannot provide any secure foundation for Commonwealth or State action, and must inevitably lead—and in fact has already led—to divergencies and inconsistencies more and more pronounced as the decisions accumulate.'

Later on, at page 154, the majority judges applied these principles. They dealt with an argument which had been advanced for the States that Section 107 of the Constitution was a provision which limited the operation of the Commonwealth industrial power; Section 107 being one which said that:

Every power of the Parliament of a Colony which has become or becomes a State shall, unless it is by this Constitution exclusively vested in the Parliament of the Commonwealth or withdrawn from the Parliament of the State, continue as at the establishment of the Commonwealth. . . .

The Court disposed of the argument based on this provision in a passage which is at once brief and explicit:

They said, 'applying these principles to the present case, the matter stands thus:

Section 51 (XXXV) is in terms so general that it extends to all industrial disputes in fact extending beyond the limits of any one State, no exception being expressed as to industrial disputes in which States are concerned. The respondents suggest only Section 107 as containing by implication a provision to the contrary. The answer is that Section 107 contains nothing which in any way either cuts down the meaning of the expression "industrial disputes" or exempts the Crown in right of a State, when party to an industrial dispute in fact, from the operation of Commonwealth legislation. Section 107 continues the previously existing powers of every State to legislate with respect to exclusive State powers, and concurrent State powers. But it is a fundamental and fatal error to read Section 107 as reserving any power from the Commonwealth that falls fairly within the explicit terms of an express grant in Section 51, as that grant is reasonably construed, unless that reservation is as explicitly stated.'

Well, sir, after this historic decision, it is not surprising that there should have been a disposition to press its effect too far; to set no limits to it.

Mr Justice Dixon (as he then was) in the *Essendon Case*, (1947) 74 C.L.R. 1 at 23, said 'There is little justification for seeking to find in the *Engineers' Case* authority for more than was decided. The importance alike of the principle there applied and of the application given to it is sufficiently great and far reaching.' He referred to the same matter in a later *Melbourne Corporation Case*, 74 C.L.R. 31, at 78–9, and said:

The prima facie rule is now that a power to legislate with regard to a given subject matter enables the Parliament to make laws which, upon that subject, affect the operations of the States and their agencies. That, as I have pointed out more than once, is the effect of the *Engineers' Case* stripped of embellishment and reduced to the form of a legal proposition. It is subject, however, to certain reservations.

Now, three reservations have been judicially noted. The first and second are that in the *Engineers' Case*, in the majority judgment the question was left open whether the principle of that case would warrant legislation affecting the exercise of 'a prerogative' of the Crown in right of a State, or dealing with 'taxation'. The majority said (at page 144):

If in any future case concerning the prerogative in the broader sense, or arising under some other Commonwealth power—for example, taxation—the extent of that power should come under consideration . . . the special nature of the power may have to be taken into account.

The third reservation is that the decision in the *Engineers' Case* did not deal with or affect the question whether the Parliament of the Commonwealth could validly enact legislation discriminating against a State or its agencies.

Now, these reservations seem to me, sir, to have a common basis. I will go over them as briefly as I can. The old doctrine of implied prohibition upon Commonwealth powers to protect the so-called 'reserved' or residuary powers of the States had been rejected as involving a complete logical inconsistency, but it still remained proper to take into account the basic fact that the Consititution had created both Commonwealth and States, had marked out their powers, and had contemplated their continued existence. In other words, *a federal structure* had been created, and the continuance of *a federal system* clearly contemplated.

I again quote Mr Justice Dixon when he said, in the *Melbourne Corporation Case* at 81,

I do not think that either under the Constitution of the United States or the British North America Act or the Commonwealth Constitution has countenance been given to the notion that the legislative powers of one Government in the system can be used in order directly to deprive another Government of powers or authority committed to it, or restrict that Government in their exercise, notwithstanding the complete overthrow of the general doctrine of reciprocal immunity of government agencies and the discrediting of the reasoning used in its justification. For that reason the distinction has been constantly drawn between a law of general application and a provision singling out governments and placing special burdens upon the exercise of powers or the fulfilment of functions constitutionally belonging to them. It is but a consequence

[43]

of the conception upon which the Constitution is framed. The foundation of the Constitution is the conception of a central Government and a number of State Governments separately organized. The Constitution predicates their continued existence as independent entities. Among them it distributes the powers of governing the country.

Now, I shall make a brief comment on each of these 'reservations'.

First of all, the prerogative of the Crown in right of the State. We do not talk about the prerogative of the Crown in one sense in Australia as one would in Great Britain, because we have 'the Crown in right of the Commonwealth' and 'the Crown in right of the State'. There are certain prerogative rights which will be exercised according to the nature of the government concerned. Now the reservation about 'the prerogative' contemplates, I think, no more than this; that there may be prerogatives exercised by State Governments, such as those related to the calling of State Parliament, the appointment of State Ministers, of State Executive Councils, the prerogative of mercy in relation to offences against State laws, and so on. It is hard to imagine that an invasion of these by the Commonwealth could be related to some specific Commonwealth power. It would certainly seem to violate the principle based upon the nature of the federal structure.

I should point out that some special considerations apply to the prerogative rights of the Commonwealth. In a recent case of *Commonwealth* v. *Cigamatic Pty. Ltd* (1962), 108 C.L.R. 372, the High Court held that the Parliament of a State has no power to control or abolish the Commonwealth's fiscal right as a Government to priority of payment of debts due to it when, in an administration of assets, those debts come into competition with debts of equal degree due to its subjects.

The company, incorporated in New South Wales, and

then in liquidation, owed the Commonwealth money under the Sales Tax Acts and the Post and Telegraphs Act. The winding up was under the State law of New South Wales, and one section of that Act in New South Wales prescribed an order of priority incompatible with the priority claimed by the Commonwealth.

The High Court decided for the Commonwealth. The Chief Justice said:

> The proposition that is implied is that an exercise of State legislative power may directly derogate from the rights of the Commonwealth with respects to its people. It is a proposition which must go deep in the nature and operation of the federal system. There can be no doubt as to the nature or the source of the right of the Commonwealth in an administration of assets to be paid in preference to subjects of the Crown if there is a competition among debts of equal degree. It springs from the nature of the Commonwealth as a government of the Queen. Therefore to treat those rights as subject to destruction or modification or qualification by the legislature of a State in a State or States must mean that under the Constitution there resides a legislative power to control legal rights and duties between the Commonwealth and its people.

He went on to say, and the majority agreed, that:

> The doctrine thus involved is a fundamental error in a constitutional principle that spreads far beyond the mere preference of debts owing to the Commonwealth.

Now the second exception: Taxation. Here, sir, I would suggest for myself that the limitations upon the Commonwealth power are (except for what I will say about discrimination later on in the third reservation) to be found expressly stated in the Constitution. And they are these:

In Section 51, sub-section ii, there is a power in the Commonwealth to make law as to 'taxation, but so as not to discriminate between States or parts of States'.

Section 99, 'The Commonwealth shall not, by any law or regulation of trade, commerce, or revenue, give preference to one State or any part thereof over another State or any part thereof'.

And in Section 114, 'A State shall not, without the consent of the Parliament of the Commonwealth . . . impose any tax on property of any kind belonging to the Commonwealth, nor shall the Commonwealth impose any tax on property of any kind belonging to a State.'

Now, that is all I wish to say on the taxation point.

Third, discrimination. Clearly, as the decisions now stand, the [general] principle is that whenever the Constitution confers a power to make laws in respect of a specific subject matter, *prima facie* it is to be understood as enabling the Parliament to make laws affecting the States and their agencies. Now, nothing was said about the subject of discrimination in the *Engineers' Case* itself. That discrimination might be significant was first suggested by the High Court in the case of *Pirrie and McFarlane* (1925), 36 C.L.R. 170. It is now well established as an exception to the general principle. Thus, if the Commonwealth, under one of its heads of power, made a law which discriminated against a State or its agency, for example, by imposing duties or obligations upon State Governments which were not imposed upon other persons or bodies, the High Court would clearly be disposed to say that this would represent a direct attack upon the existence of the States, the continued existence of which, as I have pointed out, is predicated by the federal nature of the Constitution.

On that matter the *Melbourne Corporation Case* is very much in point. I have made a brief reference to it. The Commonwealth Parliament had passed a Banking Act which precluded a bank from doing banking business for a State or any authority of a State, a term which included a local governing body set up under State law with a bank other than the Commonwealth Bank, except with the consent of the Commonwealth Treasurer. Well, the Corporation of the City of Melbourne declined to desert its regular Bank, which was not the Commonwealth Bank, and challenged the validity of the law on the ground that it was specifically directed to the States—any state or an instrumentality set up by a State—and would operate to impair the exercise by them, the States, of their function as State governments in a Federation. The Court, with only one dissentient, accepted this argument and disallowed the Act.

This is a very good example of the meaning of the 'discrimination' reservation from the rule in the *Engineers' Case*. And it gains added point when I tell you that the Commonwealth's Pay-Roll Tax legislation—is it as popular here as it is in Australia?—begun in 1941, defines 'employer' as:

> Any person who pays or is liable to pay any wages and includes,
>
> (*a*) The Crown in the right of a State;
>
> (*b*) A municipal corporation or other local governing body or a public authority constituted under any State Act.

Now, you see, there is a specific reference to the State, and the body set up by the State. But it also comes under the general description, 'any person' who pays or is liable to pay wages. The validity of that provision was once challenged, but the challenge was not pursued; no doubt for practical financial reasons. The rule of interpretation in the *Engineers' Case* operates as I would have thought fully against the

States in such a provision, for there is no discrimination against them.*

As a piece of political history, I should tell you that the then Government reacted very sharply to the High Court's decision on the Banking Act. It promptly announced that it would settle the argument by nationalizing all the Banks and creating a Government monopoly. This it proceeded to do by what it regarded as appropriate, though, as it turned out, invalid legislation, only to find at the next Election that the electors did not agree. That is how I came to be Prime Minister for the second time. So that, in the result, ladies and gentlemen, as sometimes does happen in the best regulated politics, the Government settled the issue by settling itself.

To conclude, and allowing for these reservations from the rule in the *Engineers' Case*, it is clear, I think, that the method of interpreting Commonwealth powers there approved was revolutionary, and has had and will continue to have a great influence upon the scope and weight of Commonwealth powers. And this, I remind you, as I did a fortnight ago, without any amendment of the written instrument.

In my next lecture, sir, I will pursue this into another field by talking about the defence power and the interpretation of that defence power by the High Court of Australia.

* Since I wrote these paragraphs, it has been suggested to me that a Commonwealth law taxing, say, royalties, including State royalties from mineral resources, might turn out to be invalid as against the State, on the ground that it would impair the exercise by the State of one of its constitutional functions and rights.

4

Supplementary Note on the Absence of a Bill of Rights

A	T the end of the second lecture I was asked, very reasonably, why the Australian Constitution does not contain a 'Bill of Rights'. I made a brief reply, which I now elaborate. For the more I have seen of the United States Constitution in action, and the machinery of Congress, and the judgments of the American Supreme Court, the more I have come to realize that our Constitutional differences are profound, and that our resemblances can be over-emphasized. There will be avoidable disagreements in the future unless we take the trouble to understand that there are more routes than one on the approach to the democratic heaven.

For the benefit of non-Americans, I will set out the leading provisions of the 'Bill of Rights' amendments to the American Constitution.

1. Congress shall make no law respecting an establishment of religion, or prohibiting the free exercise thereof; or abridging the freedom of speech, or of the press; or the right of the people peaceably to assemble, and to petition the Government for a redress of grievances.
2. A well-regulated militia, being necessary to the security of a free State, the right of the people to keep and bear arms, shall not be infringed.
3. No soldier shall, in time of peace, be quartered in any

[49]

house, without the consent of the owner, nor in time of war, but in a manner to be prescribed by law.

4. The right of the people to be secure in their persons, houses, papers, and effects, against unreasonable searches and seizures, shall not be violated, and no warrants shall issue, but upon probable cause, supported by oath or affirmation, and particularly describing the place to be searched, and the persons or things to be seized.

5. No person shall be held to answer for a capital, or other infamous crime, unless on a presentment or indictment of a Grand Jury, except in cases arising in the land or naval forces, or in the militia, when in actual service, in time of war or public danger; nor shall any person be subject for the same offense to be twice put in jeopardy of life or limb; nor shall be compelled in any criminal case to be a witness against himself; nor be deprived of life, liberty, or property, without due process of law; nor shall private property be taken for public use, without just compensation.

6. In all criminal prosecutions, the accused shall enjoy the right to a speedy and public trial, by an impartial jury of the State and district wherein the crime shall have been committed, which district shall have been previously ascertained by law, and to be informed of the nature and cause of the accusation; to be confronted with witness against him; to have compulsory process for obtaining witnesses in his favour, and to have the assistance of counsel for his defense.

8. Excessive bail shall not be required, nor excessive fines imposed, nor cruel and unusual punishments inflicted.

9. The enumeration in the Constitution, of certain rights shall not be construed to deny or disparage others retained by the people.

[50]

13. (1) Neither slavery nor involuntary servitude, except as a punishment for crime whereof the party shall have been duly convicted, shall exist within the United States, or any place subject to their jurisdiction.

(2) Congress shall have power to enforce this article by appropriate legislation.

14. (1) All persons born or naturalized in the United States, and subject to the jurisdiction thereof, are citizens of the United States and of the State wherein they reside. No State shall make or enforce any law which shall abridge the privileges or immunities of citizens of the United States; nor shall any State deprive any person of life, liberty, or property, without due process of law; nor deny to any person within its jurisdiction the equal protection of the laws.

15. The right of citizens of the United States to vote shall not be denied or abridged by the United States or by any State on account of race, color, or previous condition of servitude.

19. The right of citizens of the United States to vote shall not be denied or abridged by the United States or by any State on account of sex.

Compare these provisions with those of the Australian Constitution, which is notably free of such express individual guarantees. The only such provisions in the Australian Constitution are:

1. Section 51 (xxxi): The acquisition of property *on just terms* from any State or person for any purpose in respect of which the Parliament has power to make laws.
2. Section 92: (see Chapter 9).
3. Section 116: The Commonwealth shall not make any law for establishing any religion, or for imposing any religious observance, or for prohibiting the free exercise of any religion, and no religious test shall be

required as a qualification for any office or public trust under the Commonwealth.

4. Section 117: (see Appendix).

I must say, and I speak only for myself, that I am glad that the draftsmen of the Australian Constitution, though they gave close and learned study to the American Constitution and its amendments made little or no attempt to define individual liberties. They knew that, with legal definition, words can become more important than ideas. They knew that to define human rights is either to limit them—for in the long run words must be given some meaning—or to express them so broadly that the discipline which is inherent in all government and ordered society becomes impossible.

As I understand it, the Australian draftsmen had good reasons for not following the American model.

They were admirably expressed by Sir Owen Dixon, our greatest Australian authority on constitutional law, in a speech to the American Bar Association in August 1942 as follows: *Jesting Pilate* (Law Book Co. of Australia), pp. 101, 102.

The men who drew up the Australian Constitution had the American document before them; they studied it with care; they even read the standard books of the day which undertook to expound it. They all lived, however, under a system of responsible government. That is to say, they knew and believed in the British system by which the Ministers are responsible to the Parliament and must go out of office whenever they lose the confidence of the legislature. They felt therefore impelled to make one great change in adapting the American Constitution. Deeply as they respected your institutions, they found themselves unable to accept the principle by which the executive government is made independent of the legislature. Responsible government, that is, the system by which the executive is responsible to the legislature, was therefore introduced with all its necessary consequences.

In this country men have come to regard formal guarantees of life, liberty and property against invasion by government, as indispensable to a free constitution. Bred in this doctrine, you may think it strange that in Australia, a democracy if ever there was one, the cherished American practice of placing in the fundamental law guarantees of personal liberty should prove unacceptable to our constitution makers. But so it was. The framers of the Australian Constitution were not prepared to place fetters upon legislative action, except and in so far as it might be necessary for the purpose of distributing between the States and the central Government the full content of legislative power. The history of their country had not taught them the need of provisions directed to the control of the legislature itself. The working of such provisions in this country was conscientiously studied, but, wonder as you may, it is a fact that the study fired no one with enthusiasm for the principle. With the probably unnecessary exception of the guarantee of religious freedom, our constitution makers refused to adopt any part of the Bill of Rights of 1791 and *a fortiori* they refused to adopt the Fourteenth Amendment. It may surprise you to learn that in Australia one view held was that these checks on legislative action were undemocratic, because to adopt them argued a want of confidence in the will of the people. Why, asked the Australian democrats, should doubt be thrown on the wisdom and safety of entrusting to the chosen representatives of the people sitting either in the federal Parliament or in the State Parliaments all legislative power, substantially without fetter or restriction?

In our steadfast faith in responsible government and in plenary legislative powers distributed, but not controlled, you as Americans may perceive nothing better than a wilful refusal to see the light and an obstinate adherence to heresies; but we remain impenitent.

In one aspect, I should elaborate that statement. There is a basic difference between the American system of government and the system of 'responsible government' which exists both in Great Britain and Australia. For, though in both the Constitution of the United States and that of the Commonwealth of Australia the powers of the Legislature, the Executive, and the Judicature are separately stated, the truth is that in Australia (and in Great Britain) the Executive is not only responsible to the Legislature but, in its political embodiment is part of and directly responsible to the Legislature. With us, a Minister is not just a nominee of the head of the Government. He is and must be a Member of Parliament, elected as such, and answerable to Members of Parliament at every sitting. He is appointed by a Prime Minister similarly elected and open to regular question. Should a Minister do something which is thought to violate fundamental human freedom he can be promptly brought to account in Parliament. If his Government supports him, the Government may be attacked, and if necessary defeated. And if that, as it normally would, leads to a new General Election, the people will express their judgment at the polling booths.

In short, responsible government in a democracy is regarded by us as the ultimate guarantee of justice and individual rights. Except for our inheritance of British institutions and the principles of the Common Law, we have not felt the need of formality and definition.

I would say, without hesitation, that the rights of individuals in Australia are as adequately protected as they are in any other country in the world.

In America, if I may say so as a most friendly observer, there is a long history of distrust of 'official' people. As they are not directly answerable in Congress, where they do not sit, and in whose proceedings they are 'outsiders', it has been thought necessary to impose constitutional limits upon them, with the Supreme Court as the interpreter of those limits.

And as the interpretation of such provisions will be largely affected by political and social concepts, the judgments of the Supreme Court of the United States tend to possess a political flavour which is notably absent from the judgments of the High Court of Australia, as I have indicated in these lectures.

5

Growth by Judicial Interpretation
The Defence Powers of the Commonwealth

For the purpose of discussing the defence powers of the Commonwealth of Australia, I must first set out the relevant provisions of the Commonwealth Constitution. They are as follows:

Section 51, which is the principle section creating Commonwealth power, gives the Commonwealth 'power to make laws for the peace, order, and good government of the Commonwealth with respect to:

(vi) the naval and military defence of the Commonwealth and of the several States, and the control of the forces to execute and maintain the laws of the Commonwealth.

(xxxii) The control of railways with respect to transport for the naval and military purposes of the Commonwealth.

(xxxix) Matters incidental to the execution of any power vested by this Constitution in the Parliament or in either House thereof or in the government of the Commonwealth . . . or in any department or officer of the Commonwealth.'

Section 52 says that 'the Parliament shall, subject to this Constitution, have exclusive power to make laws for the peace, order, and good government of the Commonwealth with respect to:

(ii) Matters relating to any department of the public service the control of which is by this Constitution transferred to the Executive Government of the Commonwealth.'

Section 68 provides that 'The Command in Chief of the naval and military forces of the Commonwealth is vested in the Governor-General as the Queen's representative'.

Section 69 provides that 'the following departments of the public service in each State shall become transferred to the Commonwealth . . . naval and military defence'.

Section 70 says that 'In respect of matters which, under this Constitution, pass to the Executive Government of the Commonwealth, all powers and functions which at the establishment of the Commonwealth are vested in the Governor of a colony, or in the Governor of a colony with the advice of his Executive Council, or in any authority of a colony, shall vest in the Governor-General, or in the Governor-General in Council, or in the authority exercising similar powers under the Commonwealth, as the case requires'.

Section 114 provides that 'A State shall not, without the consent of the Parliament of the Commonwealth, raise or maintain any naval or military force. . . .'

Section 119 says 'The Commonwealth shall protect every State against invasion and, on the application of the Executive Government of the State, against domestic violence'.

Now, I should pause here, and say this to you. I mentioned Section 52, where certain exclusive powers are given to the Commonwealth. It must be understood that the specific powers given to the Commonwealth are, except where expressly stated to be exclusive, concurrent powers. They are concurrent because the State retains its authority to pass a law on that matter; but Section 109 of the Constitution provides that where there is a Commonwealth law on a matter within Commonwealth competence and there is a State law on the same subject-matter, then to the extent of any inconsistency between them, the Commonwealth law prevails. So, you may take it that our concurrent powers in the Commonwealth become paramount in the case of a conflict, but powers expressed to be exclusive are exclusive in the sense that the State cannot make a law about them at all.

During the First World War, the meaning of these provisions, and in particular of sub-section (vi) of Section 51 was discussed and decided by the High Court. The first case was *Farey* v. *Burvett* (1916), 21 C.L.R. 433.

I will never forget Mr. Farey, either as a lawyer or as a customer; for he sold his bread to our family in the respectable suburb of Camberwell, in Melbourne. He little knew how celebrated he was to become; not so much for his bread, though it was excellent, but for his involuntary service to legal interpretation. Under its War Precautions Act the Commonwealth had made regulations, one of which fixed the price of bread in defined localities. Did fixing the price of bread in a suburban shop fall within 'the naval and military defence' of the Commonwealth? Five of the Justices said that it did. Two dissented, saying (p. 465) 'We venture to think that they' (those words) 'extend to the raising, training and equipment of naval and military forces, to the maintenance, control and use of such forces, to the supply of arms, ammunition and other things necessary for naval and military operation, to all matters strictly ancillary to these purposes, and to nothing more'. As a matter of normal statutory interpretation there was and is much to be said for this view. Fortunately for the organization of the nation for war, and fortunately for the development of broad principles of interpretation of granted powers, it did not prevail, though some of the reasoning of the majority is so curious that one should perhaps suggest that on this legally historic occasion *salus populi suprema lex* was never quite absent from the judicial mind.

Griffith C. J., who had been one of the draftsmen of the Constitution, and who had brought a strong mind to the Bench, rather astonishingly said (p. 440): 'The words "naval" and "military" are not words of limitation, but rather of extension, showing that the subject matter includes all kinds of war-like operations. . . . In my opinion the word "defence" of itself includes all acts of such a kind as may be done in the United Kingdom . . . for the purpose of the defence of the realm, except so far as they are prohibited by other provisions of the Constitution.'

Isaacs J., having summarized the defence provisions of the Constitution, solved the whole problem in a single blow in the following words (p. 452): 'So that by the very words of the Constitution there is vested, in the most ample and absolute terms, in the Commonwealth the full powers and duty of taking every measure of defence which the circumstances may require as they present themselves to the proper organs of government, to protect this continent from foreign aggression, for maintaining its freedom—always under the British Crown—and in short for preserving its very existence as a unit of the Imperial family of nations.'

You may think that this piece of reasoning is somewhat over-charged with generous and loyal emotion. I may add that other judges were not disposed to be so absolute. But the fact is that the regulations were upheld. Thenceforward the defence power was to be interpreted, in and after two wars, as a power limited only by its dominant purpose and, of course, by any positive constitutional provisions to the contrary. Two of such provisions were brought into account in *Andrews* v. *Howell* (1941), 65 C.L.R. 255. In that case the High Court upheld the validity, under the defence power, of the *National Security (Apple and Pear Acquisition) Regulations.* *Starke J.* dissented, but agreed with the majority in finding that the regulations did not contravene Section 92* of the Constitution and that, in relation to Section 51 (xxxi)† of the Constitution, they did not provide for the acquisition of property otherwise than on just terms.‡

It has been said, in some later commentaries, that what the High Court did was to treat the defence power as, if not *sui generis*, at least occupying a special category as a 'purposive' power; the overall *purpose* being the defence of the nation, other words were to be subordinated to that end.

This was neatly put by *Higgins J.* in *Farey* v. *Burvett* at p. 459 in these words: 'To secure peace and contentment and orderly industry among the people, from whom all our national force comes, may be as valuable a war measure as the equipment of an army division.'

Many years afterwards, in the *Communist Party Case* (to which I shall refer at greater length) *Fullagar J.* put it in this way (83 C.L.R. at 253): 'The power given by Section 51 (vi) of the Constitution is given by reference to the purpose or object of the law and not by reference to some concrete subject matter.'

By no means all of the decisions have been made in relation to regulations made during the actual course of war. I would be exceeding the limits of time, and, as a judicial wit once said in my presence—though not, I hope, with reference to me—'trespassing upon eternity', if I examined a long list of

---

* Section 92 is one of the few provisions in the Australian Constitution in which broad and embracive generalizations have been expressed, of a type with which you are so familiar in the Constitution of the United States. Its operative words are that 'trade, commerce, and intercourse among the States shall be absolutely free'.

† Section 51 (xxxi) reads, 'The acquisition of property on just terms from any State or person for any purpose in respect of which the Parliament has power to make laws'.

‡ That the defence power is subject to both Sections 92 and 51 (xxxi) is now clear. *Gratwick* v. *Johnson,* 70 C.L.R.; *Dalziel's Case* 68 C.L.R. 261.

cases decided in relation to laws relating to the 'winding down' which follows a war effort. The principle was stated by *Fullagar J.* in 83 C.L.R. at 254 in words which are sufficient for my purpose:

> What I have called the secondary aspect of the defence power has so far only been invoked and expounded in connection with an actual state of war in which Australia has been involved. It has hitherto, I think, been treated in the cases as coming into existence upon the commencement or immediate apprehension of war and continuing during war and the period necessary for post-war re-adjustment. In a world of uncertain and rapidly changing international situations it may well be held to arise in some degree upon circumstances which fall short of an immediate apprehension of war. In its secondary aspect the power extends to an infinite variety of matters which could not be regarded in the normal conditions of national life as having any connection with defence.

He went on at p. 255,

> It may be that, on its true analysis, this secondary aspect of the defence power depends wholly on Section 51 (xxxix) of the Constitution. On this view, the effect of a national emergency is that the matters which I have mentioned, and very many others, become 'matters incidental to the execution' of the power of the Executive to deal with the emergency.

In the light of these decisions, many regulations were upheld, both in the First and Second World Wars. They are sufficiently exemplified by a passage from Dr Anstey Wynes's valuable book, a book to which I am much indebted, *Legislative Executive and Judicial Powers in Australia,* 3rd ed., at pp. 261–2.

Regulations fixing the prices of living or working

accommodations and securing persons in the possession of occupied premises; regulations empowering the ministerial 'declaration' of goods and services for the purposes of enabling prices to be fixed in respect thereof; regulations empowering the Treasurer to fix maximum and minimum prices of shares; regulations empowering the acquisition by the Commonwealth by Ministerial Order of apples and pears with the object of minimizing the disorganization of marketing likely to result from export difficulties arising out of the effects of the war upon shipping; regulations prohibiting the publication of advertisements of a stated character; regulations empowering tribunals to cancel or vary contracts upon satisfaction that performace was or was likely to become impossible, inequitable or unduly onerous by reason of circumstances attributable to the war or the operation of any national security regulation; regulations empowering a State Premier to require bars in licensed premises to be and be kept open during specified hours; a Ministerial Order prohibiting the carrying on of business as a master baker or bread distributor or the distribution of bread in an area to which the order applied without a licence, the order being made in pursuance of a general regulation empowering the Minister to restrict or prohibit the production, movement, distribution, sale or purchase, of articles appearing to him to be essential for the purposes of the war or the maintenance of essential supplies and services, etc.; regulations prohibiting the purchase of land without the written consent, with or without conditions, of the Treasurer whose decision was in his absolute discretion; and regulations prohibiting dealings in new motor vehicles without a permit.

These were all economic measures, which came within the broad defence purpose, but were clearly not directly either naval or military.

Other regulations were in the field of industrial labour. As *Dr Wynes* has recorded, at p. 263 :

The Commonwealth has no general power in respect of labour conditions under the Constitution. The following direct regulations of industrial conditions were, however, upheld as a valid exercise of the defence power in war time : the regulation of the employment of women for the purpose of aiding the prosecution of the war; the exercise of control in relation to all industrial disputes and industrial unrest notwithstanding the limiting provisions of Section 51 (xxxv), including the limitation of holidays to persons engaged in industry, including State servants; a regulation made by the Governor-General empowering the direction of manpower either generally or in particular cases; a regulation empowering the reference to the Arbitration Court of the question of minimum rates for female workers in industries declared vital; provision for additional holiday pay to persons employed in a defence establishment whether or not they were engaged in defence works; and a regulation requiring the consent of the Women's Employment Board to the employment of females to perform work which at any time since the beginning of the war has been performed by males.

You may well feel that, while I have described to you the expansion of the operation of the Commonwealth Parliament's defence power in two wars and in the period of 'winding down' after each of them, the effect on Commonwealth powers in times of peace could be very small.

To this view I would make two answers.

The first is that the decision in *Farey* v. *Burvett*, though made in respect of a very special kind of power, was of almost revolutionary significance. Personally, I would read it with the judgments in the *Engineers' Case* as effecting a major growth, *by interpretation*, in the powers of the Commonwealth. My reasons for saying this are that, in *Farey* v. *Burvett*, being confronted by a choice between the literal meaning of the words 'the naval and military defence of the Commonwealth', a meaning subscribed to by Justices Gavan Duffy and Rich, and an interpretation which laid all the emphasis upon the word 'defence', said that *defence* in all its aspects, military, economic, and social, was the *purpose* of the power, and that the particular words used, such as 'naval' and 'military', were of subordinate significance, the High Court decided in favour of the broad interpretation.

This was, indeed, a broad interpretation. It has been followed and applied in so many war and immediate post-war cases that it must be now taken as established beyond challenge.

The significance of the case as a guide to interpretation is therefore very great. I would find it difficult to accept the view that the defence power is completely *sui generis*, and that the methods of interpretation applied to it are not capable of being applied to other powers. I have no doubt that most of us would be reluctant to accept the view of *Isaacs J.* in *Farey* v. *Burvett* at pp. 453–4, that:

> It is the *ultimate ratio* of the nation. The defence power . . . passing into action becomes the pivot of the Constitution, because it is the bulwark of the State. Its limits then are bounded only by the requirements of self-preservation.

He even went on later to say:

> Section 92 in the most positive terms places beyond Commonwealth and State control alike the freedom of all inter-state commerce and intercourse. But though in ordinary times of peace this cannot be infringed, could it be asserted for a moment that it limits the war power?

In the case of *Andrews* v. *Howell* 65 C.L.R. 255, this view of Section 92 in relation to the defence power was clearly not followed; the Judges in that case found that the regulations challenged did not contravene Section 92—an irrelevant enquiry if Isaacs J. was right—and also found that certain acquisitions of property by virtue of the regulations did not provide for the acquisition of property otherwise than on just terms. This latter finding suggests that Section 51 (xxxi) 'The acquisition of property on just terms from any State or person for any purpose in respect of which the Parliament has power to make laws' operates in relation to the exercise of the defence power.

But the proposition that the defence power exists and can be exercised only 'subject to this Constitution' (see the opening words of Section 51) does not avoid the broad significance of the decisions. In *Andrews* v. *Howell* (1941), 65 C.L.R. at p. 27, Dixon J. stated the matter compendiously as follows: 'In dealing with that constitutional power [defence], it must be remembered that, *though its meaning does not change*, yet unlike some other powers its *application* depends upon facts, and as those facts change so may its actual *operation* as a power enabling the legislature to make a law. The existence and character of hostilities against the Commonwealth are *facts* which will determine the extent of the operation of the power.' (*The italics are my own.*)

The great point to be emphasized is that *Dixon J.* was saying, and none of his colleagues in 1941 would have disagreed, that the *meaning* of the power, the meaning first assigned to it in *Farey* v. *Burvett*, would continue to be its meaning even in a period of undisturbed peace, though its applicability to specific circumstances might be very different.

The defence cases, therefore, establish as valid and continuing a broad interpretation of Commonwealth defence powers, an interpretation which in any appropriate case subordinates the particular expression to the *broad purposes* of the power.

A similar approach was made by the High Court in R. v.

Brislan 54 C.L.R. 262, where the Court (Dixon J. dissenting) dealt with the Commonwealth's power in relation to 'postal, telegraphic, telephonic, and other like services' and decided that the power extended to the control of radio broadcasting on the view that a generic and not a specific interpretation was appropriate.

My first answer is therefore that the defence cases have had and will have a large impact, an impact based upon the method of interpreting *the power* as distinct from its special applications in time of war, upon the whole process of interpreting the legislative powers of the Commonwealth. The *Engineers' Case* dealt with the other aspect of the matter; the power being broadly interpreted, are the States or their instrumentalities excluded from its operation? I have dealt already with this in my examination of that great case.

But there is a *second consequence* of the defence cases which, while it possesses no technical legal significance, has, in my opinion and experience, had political consequences which are relevant to my thesis.

In two great wars, the defence power of the Commonwealth has, with judicial sanction, operated over an enormous area of domestic life; in the First World War, under the War Precautions Act, in the Second, under the National Security Act. It is not always realized, even in your great country, that in these wars Australia had many more than a million men under arms, and suffered very great casualties. In the Second World War, the enemy came close to our shores, and was, with the powerful intervention of your own forces, repelled. A general mobilization of manpower and physical resources occurred. The civilian population became familiar with Commonwealth authority in what had always been State or municipal functions. Food, clothing, petrol, motor transport, investments, labour, manufacturing, were all Commonwealth-controlled; while personal and company taxes very properly rose to the highest point in our history. If permits or licences for goods were needed, it was a Commonwealth official who dealt with the matter. The Commonwealth, indeed, became all-pervasive, and was hated or loved, according to individual tastes and circumstances. To enable the vast burden of income taxation to be equitably distributed, what was and is called Uniform Tax was introduced; a matter with which I will deal in another lecture.

When the war ended with our common victory, it was possible for me and people like me concerned with understanding and influencing (or even evoking) public opinion, to detect in it certain currents which varied in strength from one period to another.

The first current was one of anxiety to be quit of controls as soon as possible; this might be described as in one aspect a movement against Commonwealth power. In its extreme and urgent forms, this opinion had to be resisted by the then Government, for the good reason that, with the abstraction of so many hundreds of thousands of people from civilian to defence occupations, civil production was down and material resources depleted, while the virtual forcing of saving and investment into public securities—war loans in particular—had put into the hands of the people a very large volume of purchasing power which, if suddenly set free, could have produced a dangerous inflation at the very time when so much industrial reconstruction work had to be done. The circumstances were understood by most people. I say this for the very human and therefore pardonable reason that it was my own view. Yet it is strange for me to recall that the *Chifley* Labour Government, in the very early post-war years, was preoccupied by fears of a slump and heavy unemployment; a conception which made its prolonged retention of almost all of its controls a little hard to follow, though capable of support, within reason, on the grounds I have indicated. The Government conducted the dismantling process slowly, but won the 1946 Election handsomely. Thereafter, the feeling grew that the process was too slow; that the Government was, as a Socialist government, 'control-minded', and wanted controls for their own sake. This feeling played some part in the defeat of the Government in the Election of 1949, which imposed my services upon the nation until early in 1966, when, in breach of normal political practice, I retired voluntarily.

Now so far, the facts I have referred to would suggest an attitude of growing hostility to Commonwealth powers. They go some way towards explaining the defeat in 1944—while the war was still on—of the Labour Government's fourteen proposals for added peacetime power, and the defeat in 1948 of that Government's proposal to give the Commonwealth power over 'rents and prices'. I dealt with these in my first lecture.

Had this been the only current of opinion, it could be said, with much good sense, that the growth of Commonwealth activities under the expansive interpretation of the defence powers would operate in the public mind to restrain any movement, visible or invisible, towards the aggregation of further powers in the hands of the Commonwealth. Indeed, nothing I have said should be taken to deny that this current is still running and that we shall see its effects for years to come.

But there has been and is a cross-current, perceptible but of uncertain strength. Let me describe it to you.

The compulsion to 'go to the Commonwealth' during the war and immediate post-war period has tended to breed new habits of thought. Organizations and people have developed the habit of 'going to the Commonwealth' for the satisfaction of a great variety of needs or demands, even though the problems involved may clearly be within the normal jurisdiction of the States and not within the peacetime jurisdiction of the Commonwealth. All of these numerous requests are, in my experience, based either upon the proposition that, for example, the works involved are works of 'national' significance—I received many requests for the Commonwealth financing of small town water supplies on this somewhat assertive ground—or upon the proposition that as the Commonwealth controls income tax and loan raising for public works, a matter which I will examine in later lectures, it should be willing to accept financial responsibility for matters in relation to which it has no legislative or executive authority. I have on many occasions publicly, but I fear vainly, pointed out that this process has dangers for the States and local authorities. I have said that there is inherent in it a danger to the preservation of federalism; that if the practice of seeking to impose all responsibility upon the Commonwealth becomes inveterate, and if Commonwealth Governments yield to it, the day will come when the Commonwealth will say that powers must be matched with responsibilities if the Commonwealth is to go on being the universal provider.

This is indeed, or at least may prove to be, a powerful cross-current which may turn Australian thoughts towards increased Commonwealth powers after all.

Before I conclude, I should make a special reference to a more recent but very interesting and important decision.

The extent and character of the defence power in a period of ostensible peace, but with grave international apprehension, were discussed in the case of *Australian Communist Party* v. *Commonwealth* (1950–51), 83 C.L.R. p. 1.

The case arose in this fashion. It was a time of great international tension both in the West and in the Far East; United Nations forces, including Australian troops, were confronting Communist forces in Korea. My Government, in an endeavour to outlaw the Communist Party, and to guard against evasion of that outlawing, had secured the passage through Parliament of the Communist Party Dissolution Act 1950.

It was an elaborate Act, with a lengthy preamble. The preamble recited the Marx-Lenin revolutionary objectives of the Australian Communist Party; its subversive activities; its integration with world communism; its damaging activities in key industries vital to the security and defence of Australia; and the necessity, for such security and defence, that the Party should be dissolved with certain consequences.

Whatever the legal effect of the preamble might turn out to be, it certainly expressed formally the judgment of Parliament.

The enacting provisions of the Act were elaborate. In substance they declared the Australian Communist Party to be an unlawful association and, by force of the Act, dissolved it and vested its property in a receiver. As Communist bodies, like others, can change their names easily, and in any event take protean and sometimes outwardly orthodox forms, the Act went on to apply itself to defining the tests by which such substituted or allied bodies could be identified. In the same section it provided:

(2) Where the Governor-General is satisfied that a body of persons is a body of persons to which this section applies and that the continued existence of that body of persons would be prejudicial to the security and defence of the Commonwealth or to the execution or maintenance of the Constitution or of the laws of the Commonwealth, the Governor-General may, by instrument published in the *Gazette*, declare that body of persons to be an unlawful association.

(3) The Executive Council shall not advise the Governor-General to make a declaration under the last preceding sub-section unless the material upon which the advice is founded has first been considered by a committee consisting of the Solicitor-General, the Secretary to the Department of Defence, the Director-General of Security,

[70]

and two other persons appointed by the Governor-General.

(4) A body of persons declared to be an unlawful association under sub-section (2) of this section may, within twenty-eight days after the publication of the declaration in the *Gazette*, apply to the appropriate court to set aside the declaration, on the ground that the body is not a body to which this section applies.

Corresponding provisions were made about 'persons'.

The validity of these provisions became the central issue in the litigation which followed.

The High Court, *Latham C. J.* dissenting, found these provisions invalid, as being not warranted by the defence power.

This was not because the defence power could not apply in circumstances which fell short of actual hostilities, nor was it based on a denial of the power of the Commonwealth to protect itself against violent or subversive attack. Indeed, on the latter point, *Dixon J.* said (p. 188):

I take the view that the power to legislate against subversive conduct has a source in principle that is deeper or wider than a series of combinations of the words of Section 51 (xxxix) with those of other constitutional powers. I prefer the view adopted in the United States, which is stated in Black's *American Constitutional Law* (1910), 2nd Ed., S. 153, p. 210, as follows:

. . . it is within the necessary power of the federal government to protect its own existence and the unhindered play of its legitimate activities. And to this end, it may provide for the punishment of treason, the suppression of insurrection or rebellion, and for the putting down of all individual or concerted attempts to obstruct or interfere with the discharge of the proper business of government. . . .

It seems to me that the real essence of the decision in this case is to be found in these points :

(*a*) . . . But, whatever may be the general position, it seems to me that it would be contrary to principle to allow even prima facie probative force to recitals of facts upon which the power to make the law in question depends. It is, as I have said, clearly impossible to allow them conclusive force, because to do so would be to say that Parliament could recite itself into a field which was closed to it.

(Per *Fullagar J.* p. 264)

(*b*) The validity of a law or of an administrative act done under a law cannot be made to depend on the opinion of the law-maker, or the person who is to do the act, that the law or the consequence of the act is within the constitutional power upon which the law in question itself depends for its validity.

(Per *Fullagar J.* p. 258)

(*c*) If the Act had forbidden a particular course of conduct or created particular offences depending on facts so that the connection or want of connection with a subject matter of federal legislative power would appear from the nature of the provision, the position could be different. But the Act dealt with the Australian Communist Party directly, and in the case of affiliated or derivative organizations and persons empowered the Executive to act directly.

(See Per *Dixon J.* 183)

It is thus apparent that in committing to the Executive Council an authority to say whether the continued existence of a body or the activities of a person are prejudicial to the security or defence of the Commonwealth, the sub-sections provide a most uncertain criterion depending on matters of degree. However much care and restraint there might be in the use of the power, the likelihood would remain very great of matters being considered prejudicial to security and defence which could not possibly be made the subject of legislation. Unlike the power conferred by the National Security Act 1939–43 '(the general wartime Act)' the present power is administrative and not legislative, it is not directed to the conduct of an existing war, and its exercise is not examinable and is not susceptible of testing by reference to the constitutional power above which it cannot validly rise' *Dixon J.* pp. 185–6.

And so the Act was found *ultra vires*.

This case is of supreme interest because, while it recognizes quite explicitly the nation's inherent right of self-defence, and does not deny the application of the defence power under circumstances of tension falling short of actual war, it sets limits to the extent to which Parliament may legislate on the basis of its own opinion, or give wide purely discretionary authority to the Executive, or seek to deal with people or organizations *as such* without reference to objective standards of conduct or behaviour.

Kitto J. put this last point with his usual precision when he said at p. 278 that 'There is an essential difference between, on the one hand, a law providing for the dissolution of associations as to which specified facts exist, and, on the other hand, a law providing specially for the dissolution of a particular association'.

I described the later history of this matter in my first lecture. The limitations upon the defence power had been examined and authoritatively declared by the High Court. But the power itself remains most significant in any analysis of the over-all problem.

In my succeeding lectures, I will examine the growth of Commonwealth power in the financial, economic, and other fields.

6

The Growth of the Financial Power of the Commonwealth with particular reference to State Grants and Uniform Taxation

THIS lecture will tell the strange story of how the Commonwealth's power to give money to the States led to the Commonwealth's monopoly of income taxation.

The saying in Holy Writ—'The Lord giveth, and the Lord taketh away; Blessed be the name of the Lord'—is, in material terms, right in point.

I began by setting out the source and nature of the Commonwealth's power to give money to the States.

Section 96 of the Commonwealth Constitution reads as follows:

> During a period of ten years after the establishment of the Commonwealth and thereafter until the Parliament otherwise provides, the Parliament may grant financial assistance to any State on such terms and conditions as the Parliament thinks fit.

An earlier section, Section 87, known as the Braddon Clause and sometimes called, offensively, the 'Braddon Blot', said:

> During a period of ten years after the establishment of the Commonwealth and thereafter until the Parliament otherwise provides, of the net revenue of the Common-

wealth from duties of customs and of excise not more than one fourth shall be applied annually by the Commonwealth towards its expenditure.

The balance was to go for the benefit of the States.

Each of these provisions reflected some of the hopes and fears of the federating colonies. Section 87 was based upon what was soon discovered to be a starry-eyed expectation that the new Commonwealth Parliament and Government would be cheap. Remembering my own last Commonwealth Budget of over £2,500 million, I refrain from further comment. However, Section 87 came to an end by virtue of Section 3 of the Surplus Revenue Act 1910, which expressly terminated the operation of the Braddon Clause.

Section 96 was based upon fears, not hopes, and was, it would appear, originally designed to be temporary.

As part of the bargaining process which went on before the Constitution was finally adopted, this section was put in because it was thought that some of the federating colonies, now to become States, could suffer disabilities; particularly in what I may call the transitional period, before the new order settled down. 'During a period of ten years' suggests this. The express power of the new Parliament to alter or cancel the provision after ten years supports the suggestion.

Well, now, under Section 96, for a start, and after a certain interval of time, the Commonwealth Parliament had a special Act about State grants, and this applied to three states out of the six, the three financially smaller States— West Australia, South Australia, Tasmania. We set up the State Grants Commission and the State Grants Commission would sit each year in these individual States and then bring down a recommendation as to how many million pounds ought to be paid to each in order to remove some of their disabilities, particularly when compared with the more rich and powerful states in the East.

Well, that went on for some time (except that South Australia later ceased to be a claimant) and nobody disapproved of it.

But now, contrary to expectations, Section 96 (unlike 87) has achieved a permanent character and is employed for purposes which I venture to believe were never contemplated by the original draftsmen. For the Section has become a major, and flexible, instrument for enlarging the boundaries of Commonwealth action; or, to use realistic terms, Commonwealth power.

The High Court's wide interpretation of the Section was made laconically, in *Victoria* v. *The Commonwealth* (1926), 38 C.L.R. 399. I was counsel for the unsuccessful plaintiffs.

The case concerned the *Federal Aid Roads Act* of 1926, which gave statutory force to an agreement between the Commonwealth and each of the States; the agreement set out a plan for the construction of roads by State and Commonwealth. The roads included main developmental roads, trunk roads and arterial roads. Whatever a State did was subject to the approval of the Commonwealth, which, it must be remembered, has no general road-making powers except within its territories, or for purposes of defence.

Curiously enough, the Act itself, as *Dixon C.J.* pointed out many years later in *Victoria* v. *Commonwealth* 99 C.L.R. at p. 605, 'did not express its reliance on Section 96 either in terms or by reference to the grant of financial assistance'.

My argument for the plaintiffs was that the Act was invalid because it was in substance a law relating to road-making and not a law for granting financial aid to the States. The phrase 'such terms and conditions' I submitted, must be read consistently with the rest of the Constitution, with its demarcation of powers between Commonwealth and States, and should not be read as creating what could be described as a new Commonwealth power. In short, the phrase in question should be given a restricted meaning, restricted to the imposition of financial terms.

This argument was dismissed out of hand by a unanimous Court, at a time when unanimity was *not* one of its notable characteristics. The entire judgment was:

> The Court is of opinion that the Federal Aid Roads Act No. 46 of 1926 is a valid enactment.
>
> It is plainly warranted by the provisions of Section 96 of the Constitution, and not affected by those of Section 99 or any other provisions of the Constitution, so that exposition is unnecessary.

This made it abruptly clear that if a Commonwealth law is one providing for a grant to a State, the terms which may be attached to that grant are matters entirely within the jurisdiction of the Commonwealth Parliament. Many years later, in *Victoria* v. *Commonwealth* 99 C.L.R. at p. 606, *Dixon C.J.* summarized the effect of the Federal Aid Roads Case decision as follows:

> The validity of the legislation was upheld by this Court as authorised by s. 96. This means that the power conferred by that provision is well exercised although (1) the State is bound to apply the money specifically to an object that has been defined, (2) the object is outside the powers of the Commonwealth, (3) the payments are left to the discretion of the Commonwealth Minister, (4) the money is provided as the Commonwealth's contribution to an object for which the State is also to contribute funds. Road-making no doubt may have been conceived as a function of the State so that to provide money for its performance must amount to financial assistance to the State. But only in this way was there 'assistance'.

I now turn to the story of how this lively and continuing

power to 'grant financial assistance' came to increase the Commonwealth's taxation field.

In 1942, in what was a very critical period of the war for Australia, with the Japanese attacks on New Guinea and with the crucial battle of the Midway Islands just over, the then Government of the Commonwealth of Australia introduced a series of measures simultaneously. One of them became the States Grants (Income Tax Reimbursement) Act of 1942; one was the Income Tax (Wartime Arrangements) Act of 1942; the third, the Income Tax Assessment Act of 1942; and the fourth, the Income Tax Act of 1942. The legislation was elaborately debated in Parliament at a time when I was a Private Member of the Opposition, though I had for some time been Prime Minister. In effect, the measures proposed could be summarized in this way. The scheme of Acts did not say that the States were not to impose Income Tax, but said that the States should be deprived of the officials, officers and equipment by means of which they, at that time, assessed and collected income tax; that the Commonwealth would impose an income tax that would raise not only all that the Commonwealth needed but also an additional £34 million to meet the then requirements of the States; that any State that refrained from imposing income tax should receive the indicated financial assistance from the Commonwealth; that any State that imposed income tax would not receive this financial assistance; and that any State that persisted in imposing income tax should not collect any of it until the Commonwealth had been paid its tax in full. Now there was great substantial merit in this scheme, as I think most of us conceded. There was a tremendous war effort, and the rates of taxation needed to be very, very high if the financial requirements of the war effort were to be supplied. There was also, as the then Prime Minister Mr Curtin pointed out, some need for equality of sacrifice on the part of the taxpayers at a time when so many men, many hundreds of thousands in total, were engaged in operations of war. There had been a couple of conferences with State Governments to see whether some scheme, agreeable to them, might be worked out. The conferences had failed. The current position was that each State had its own taxing powers and exercised them, and that the Commonwealth also levied (*inter alia*) income tax. But each State differed from every other State. For example, in my home State of Victoria, which had been fairly conservative in finance, State income tax was comparatively low. On the other hand, in a State like Queensland, for a variety of reasons, State tax was relatively high. Now this state of affairs produced clear difficulties when the war came and when Commonwealth income tax had obviously to be progressively and steeply increased. It would have turned out, if the Commonwealth had proposed a rate of Common-wealth income tax adequate to the circumstances, that although taxpayers in Victoria would have a little money left, many taxpayers in Queensland, particularly in certain higher income brackets, would be paying tax at more than 20*s*. in the £. Or, should I say, more than 100 cents in the dollar!

Under these circumstances, the Government decided that the only way of producing adequate resources plus some equity of treatment was to take steps to get rid of State income tax and to substitute for it a Commonwealth income tax which would of constitutional necessity operate without discrimination as between one State and another. Now how could this be done?. The Commonwealth, it is true, has its wide power of taxation, in Section 51, sub-section (ii) of the Constitution. But each State had *its* powers of taxation, because the Commonwealth power was not exclusive; it was concurrent. The scheme devised was that the Common-wealth would not attempt directly to deprive the State of its power of taxation, its constitutional power of taxation, because obviously it could not. But it was decided that the

Commonwealth should impose rates of tax which, while satisfying the requirements of the nation for purposes of defence, would leave no real room for the imposition of what would be additional income tax by the States. In order to compensate for this serious loss of revenue, the Commonwealth decided that it would make to each State, under Section 96 of the Constitution, a grant of an amount which was specifically indicated in the legislation and which would no doubt in the future be, and was in fact, increased from time to time. The legislation sought to get over the constitutional problem by providing that if a State wished to receive this tax reimbursement, as it was called, it could do it only by agreeing not to levy income tax of its own. The other aspects of the scheme I have already referred to.

Now this scheme involved in a very acute fashion the operation of Section 96, and brought up into sharp relief the relative financial positions of Commonwealth and State. In the Parliament, rather boldly but, as it turned out, wrongly, I said that the substance of the legislation was to compel the States to forgo their right to levy income taxation. I said that although the Statutes were so drafted as to indicate that an inducement was to be offered to the States to forgo their own taxation, the truth in substance was that they were being compelled. I think there was some historic support for my proposition, because I have always believed that the highwaymen on Hounslow Heath who negotiated with people in coaches about their jewellery were no doubt giving them a choice—'your jewellery or your life'—but in reality they were depriving them of all choice whatever. They were exercising a form of compulsion.

If I may engage in a digression for a moment, it is not without interest that when the legislation came to be tested, as it was in the case of *South Australia* v. *The Commonwealth*, 65 C.L.R. 373, Mr Justice Starke stated his view that the object of the Act or the Acts was not merely to grant financial assistance to the States but that there was linked up in it an object and an end inconsistent with the limited grant of power given by Section 96, namely, making the Commonwealth the sole effective taxing authority in respect of incomes and compensating the States for the resulting loss. He went on to say that the argument that the States Grants Act left a free choice to the States, offered an inducement but deprived them of and interfered with no constitutional power was (and I use his words) 'specious but unreal'. He went on to say that it didn't meet the substance of the States' position, which was that the condition of the Act related to a matter in respect to which the Commonwealth had no constitutional power whatever, and yet by force of the condition the grant of assistance to the States was withdrawn unless they complied with its terms. He concluded by saying— I quote his words—'the real object of the position is that already stated, and it is in my judgment neither contemplated by nor sanctioned by the Constitution and in particular by Section 96 thereof. As I have said, all State legislation and functions might ultimately be so controlled and supervised.'

This powerful subsequent support for the view I had expressed in Parliament would have given me even greater legal comfort if it had not been the support of a dissentient judge; the majority took the other view. They said that as there was no actual coercion but only a rather powerful persuasion, what was done was done rightly within the taxation power of the Commonwealth and within the power of the Commonwealth to make grants to the States under Section 96, and to annex conditions at the discretion of the Commonwealth Parliament.

The decision of the High Court is of outstanding significance and deserves some citation. The first Uniform Tax decision was in *South Australia* v. *The Commonwealth* 65 C.L.R. 373. At p. 374 the headnote reads:

[81]

The Income Tax Act 1942 and the States Grants (Income Tax Reimbursement) Act 1942 are respectively within the powers of the Commonwealth Parliament to make laws with respect to taxation and to grant financial assistance to any State, notwithstanding the condition of abstinence from imposing income tax attached to such grants under the last-mentioned Act. The two Acts mentioned, whether considered separately, together, or in conjuction with section 31 of the Income Tax Assessment Act 1942 and the Income Tax (Wartime Arrangements) Act 1942, are not invalid as being legislation directed towards destroying or weakening the constitutional functions or capacities of the States or as involving discrimination contrary to sec. 51 (ii) of the Constitution or preference contrary to sec. 99.

At p. 415, *Latham C.J.* said:

It is now necessary to deal with the far-reaching and fundamental general objection which is made to the Tax Act considered in association with the other Acts, but which is particularly directed against the Grants Act.

This objection is based upon the following principle which, it is argued, applies to all Commonwealth legislative powers, namely—the Commonwealth cannot direct its legislative powers towards destroying or weakening the constitutional functions or capacities of a State. (A corresponding rule should, it is said, be applied in favour of the Commonwealth as against the States.) In another form the principle is said to be that the Commonwealth cannot use its legislative powers to destroy either 'the essential governmental functions' or 'the normal activities' of a State.

He then went on to say (pp. 416–17)

The Act does not purport to deprive the State Parliament

[82]

of the power to impose an income tax. The Commonwealth Parliament cannot deprive any State of that power: see Constitution secs. 106, 107. Notwithstanding the Grants Act a State Parliament could at any time impose an income tax. The State would then not benefit by a grant under the Act, but there is nothing in the Grants Act which could make the State income tax legislation invalid.

The Grants Act offers an inducement to the State Parliaments not to exercise a power the continued existence of which is recognised—the power to impose income tax. The States may or may not yield to this inducement, but there is no legal compulsion to yield.

The Commonwealth may properly induce a State to exercise its powers (e.g., the power to make roads: see *Victoria* v. *The Commonwealth* (*supra*), by offering a money grant. So also the Commonwealth may properly induce a State by the same means to abstain from exercising its powers. For example, the Commonwealth might wish to exercise the powers given by the Constitution, sec. 51 (xiii) and (xiv) to legislate with respect to banking, other than State banking, and insurance, other than State insurance. The Commonwealth might wish to set up some federal system of banking or insurance without any State competition. If the States were deriving revenue from State banking or State insurance they might be prepared to retire from such activities upon receiving what they regarded as adequate compensation. The Commonwealth could properly, under Commonwealth legislation, make grants to the States upon condition of them so retiring. The States could not abdicate their powers by binding themselves not to re-enter the vacated field, but if the Commonwealth, aware of this possibility, was prepared to pay money to a State which in fact gave up its system of State banking or insurance, there could be no objection on this ground to the validity of the Commonwealth law which authorized the payment.

But the position is radically different, it is urged, if the so-called inducement practically amounts to coercion. Admittedly the Commonwealth Parliament could not pass a law compelling a State to surrender the power to tax incomes or prohibiting the exercise of that power by a State. Equally, it is said, the Commonwealth cannot lawfully make an offer of money to a State which, under the conditions which actually exist, the State cannot, on political or economic grounds, really refuse.

The identification of a very attractive inducement with legal compulsion is not convincing. Action may be brought about by temptation—by offering a reward—or by compulsion. But temptation is not compulsion.

And again on pp. 422–3 :

In this case the plaintiffs do not rely on any express provision in the Commonwealth Constitution for the purpose of showing that the Tax Act and the Grants Act, as well as the other Acts considered together with them, are invalid. They rely upon the alleged implied prohibition as to non-interference by the Commonwealth with State constitutional functions, capacities or activities. They point to secs. 106 and 107 of the Constitution, which have already been quoted. These sections, however, do not confer any powers upon a State or upon a State Parliament. They preserve existing powers, but, as to State Constitutions (sec. 106) 'subject to the "(Commonwealth)" Constitution', and, as to State legislative powers (sec. 107) only after withdrawals and exclusions effected by the Constitution, and then subject to the effect of overriding Commonwealth laws where the Commonwealth Parliament has power to legislate (sec. 109). These provisions cannot be relied upon to limit by either express or implied prohibition any provision conferring powers upon the Commonwealth. They do make it clear that the Commonwealth possesses only the powers granted by the Constitution. But they do not limit the sphere or restrict the operation of the powers which are so granted.

And finally, at pp. 423–4:

Thus the principle for which the plaintiffs contend must be applied, if at all, in protection of all that a State chooses to do, and it must mean that Commonwealth legislation cannot be directed to weaken or destroy any State function or activity whatsoever.

But it cannot be denied that Commonwealth legislation may be valid though it does in fact weaken or destroy, and even is intended to weaken or destroy, some State activity. Sec. 109 shows that this must be so in many cases. Commonwealth laws have in fact put an end to the existence of State Courts of Bankruptcy and State Patent, Trade Mark and Copyright Departments. The Commonwealth laws are not invalid on that account. They have produced the results stated just because they are valid.

As a matter of history, I should point out to you that this legislation was supported by the Commonwealth in the High Court, not only under the taxation power and under Section 96, but also under the defence power. This was intelligible, because at that time it was in contemplation that the legislation would have a temporary operation. Indeed, it was expressed to continue to operate until the end of the financial year in which the war came to an end. But in due course, in 1946, further legislation was passed giving the scheme permanency, thereby resting it squarely on peacetime powers and not on the defence power of the Commonwealth. Years afterwards, this was attacked by the State of Victoria, but the High Court in the second *Uniform Tax*

Case, affirmed with one minor exception the substance of what it had decided in 1942.

The second Uniform Tax case, *Victoria* v. *Commonwealth* (1957), 99 C.L.R. 575, decided unanimously that the States Grants (Tax Reimbursement) Act 1946–48 was a valid enactment, finding its bases in Section 96 of the Constitution. Sir Owen Dixon, who did not participate in the first Uniform Tax case, had become Chief Justice, and some special interest attached to his opinion. At p. 605, he summarized the effect of Section 96 as follows:

> It is apparent that the power to grant financial assistance to any State upon such terms and conditions as the Parliament thinks fit is susceptible of a very wide construction in which few if any restrictions can be implied. For the restrictions could only be implied from some conception of the purpose for which the particular power was conferred upon the Parliament or from some general constitutional limitations upon the powers of the Parliament which otherwise an exercise of the power given by sec. 96 might transcend. In the case of what may briefly be described as coercive powers it may not be difficult to perceive that limitations of such a kind must be intended. But in sec. 96 there is nothing coercive. It is but a power to make grants of money and to impose conditions on the grant, there being no power of course to compel acceptance of the grant and with it the accompanying term or condition.
>
> There has been what amounts to a course of decisions upon sec. 96 *all amplifying the power and tending to a denial of any restriction upon the purpose of the appropriation or the character of the condition.*

Later he said:

> Once the interpretation is accepted in full which the

decisions in *Victoria* v. *The Commonwealth* and in *Moran's case* (61 C.L.R. 735, 63 C.L.R. 338) combine to place upon the section it becomes difficult indeed to find safe ground for saying that the condition of the grant of financial assistance may not be that a particular form of tax shall not be imposed by the State. . . . In short the result of my consideration of the two prior decisions upon sec. 96 has been to convince me that the decision of the majority of the Court with respect to the Tax Reimbursement Act in *South Australia* v. *The Commonwealth* was but an extension of the interpretation already placed upon sec. 96 of the Constitution. The three decisions certainly harmonize and they combine to give to sec. 96 a consistent and coherent interpretation and *they each involve the entire exclusion of the limited operation which might have been assigned to the power as an alternative.*

Fullagar J., who had not been in the first case, was equally clear, at p. 656 :

I can see no real reason for limiting in any way the nature of the conditions which may be imposed. It may be said that, if a condition calls for State action, the action must be action of which the State is constitutionally capable. But I can see no reason for otherwise limiting the power to appropriate for payment to a State subject to a condition.

(*Fullagar J.* was a great lawyer, and a close personal friend who died too young. I sometimes wonder whether, in writing these words, he recalled, with a whimsical smile, that prior to the Federal Aid Roads decision and before the subject had been illuminated by a course of judicial decision, he and I had jointly written as our opinion that we were 'disposed to regard the terms and conditions mentioned in sec. 96 as being financial terms and conditions and not such terms or conditions as would produce in result a disturbance or alteration of the Constitutional distribution of powers')

In short terms, it seems clear that there is complete judicial approval of the following propositions:

(a) The Commonwealth, by offering a money grant, may properly induce a State to exercise its powers in a particular way.

(b) It may, by offering a money grant, induce a State to abstain from exercising one or more of its powers.

(c) It can, in such ways, 'induce', but it cannot compel.

The whole run of the decisions amplifies the power residing in sec. 96, and denies any restrictions upon either the purpose of the grant or the character of the stipulated conditions.

This broad interpretation of the power has, I think, been of considerable, if unexpected, practical value to the States, though it has undoubtedly added greatly to the financial (and therefore political) predominance of the Commonwealth. But I believe the overall results to have some good elements. A very recent example is the system of grants to the States for State universities. This is a development which probably was not foreseen in 1901, or even at a much later date than that.

These grants, which were begun in my own time as Prime Minister, are, as recommendations to Government, worked out in detail, and for specific purposes, by the Commonwealth Universities Commission, and call for supplementary contributions by the States.

The whole development is one which has affected what was then thought to be the federal distribution of powers between the national Parliament, which had been granted no general power over education, which remained a State function, and the Parliaments of the States. But it undoubtedly has had the effect of saving the State universities from financial disaster, and of enabling new universities to be established. The whole matter is a very good illustration of how something which was not anticipated in the Constitution when it was first enacted can come into existence by judicial interpretation and the inexorable demands of new circumstances.

In other respects, Section 96 has been used to enable the Commonwealth to assist States in carrying out developmental works, such as roads and ports and railways outside the limits of Loan Council programmes.

Since then, what has been called uniform tax—that is to say, the exclusive operation of the Commonwealth in the income tax field—has continued to be a feature of the relations between the Commonwealth and States in the financial field.

I say this in no gloating Commonwealth fashion. I am a Federalist. I subscribe to the sound political principle that governments exercising independent powers should, if possible, have the responsibility for raising the revenues needed for such exercise. Uniform taxation, as I have described it, cuts across this principle.

But historic facts have a certain inexorable logic of their own. As Edmund Burke once pointed out, virtue which is not practicable is spurious. The problems of a scattered nation do not readily lend themselves to easy solutions. Thus, I have explained how the circumstances of the Second World War constituted the *causa causans* of uniform taxation. But the *causa sine qua non* was manifesting itself before the war. As I have pointed out, the various States had quite disparate tax rates. This fact arose from their quite different taxable capacities, depending on their degree of industrialization, the nature of their soil and rainfall, the volume of their productivity and of their business activities. It was partly for this reason that, as I indicated earlier, as far back as 1933, the Commonwealth Grants Commission was set up to recommend special grants to several of the less-developed States by way of some compensation for their disabilities.

This system has been continued, but it cannot be regarded as having much more than a marginal effect. I see now that the day was bound to come when a more comprehensive scheme of national taxation and equitable distribution would be needed. However, when I came back into office at the end of 1949, I still hoped that the principle I have just stated might somehow be restored on an equitable basis. Over a period of years thereafter I several times invited the States at Premiers' Conferences to indicate whether they wanted their income taxing powers back, and if so, on what terms. Well, the result in a Special Conference in 1953 was quite interesting.

We found a certain amount of common ground. The interests of the taxpayer should be recognized by having uniform tax assessment laws and preserving the valuable simplicity of having *one* income return and *one* document of assessment which would specify Commonwealth tax and State tax in separate columns. But there was one major matter on which agreement was not reached and, I confess with regret, seems unlikely ever to be reached. The great practical question was—to what extent should the Commonwealth reduce its own income tax to make room for the imposition of State Income Tax? The State of New South Wales—the 'mother State'—indicated that it would like its income tax powers back, but attached conditions to that offer which would have been completely impossible for the Commonwealth. In short, their Premier said that if the Commonwealth would vacate the income tax field to the extent of twice the current reimbursement to the States he would be agreeable to the restoration of their own taxing activities to the States. What this meant was this. The tax reimbursement payable that year by the Commonwealth to the States was £136 million. The New South Wales Premier wanted the Commonwealth to reduce its income tax by twice that amount! This means that the proposal was that we, the Commonwealth, should not only vacate the field to the extent to which we were then in effect collecting on behalf of the States, but that we should also reduce our remaining tax yield by an approximately similar amount. The pleasing purpose, expressly stated by the Premier of New South Wales, was that he would like to be able to accompany his resumption of State taxing power by some tax reduction! The cold fact that, to carry on the national services, we would be compelled into either a steep increase in Income or other Commonwealth taxes or a large recourse to inflationary finance through the Reserve Bank was, he thought, no concern of his. Well this, of course, was from the Commonwealth's point of view quite hopeless. Another State had a similar view, though perhaps not so extreme. Western Australia and Tasmania, which are both States who receive each year special grants from the Commonwealth, each said quite firmly, but understandably, 'We do not want our taxing powers back'. I think that in reality the one State that thought and said it wanted them back was the State of Victoria. But after two or three discussions at Premiers' Conferences, it became quite clear that no State really wanted its taxing powers back on terms which any Commonwealth Government could accept, and that consequently uniform tax, so called, must now be regarded for better or for worse as a permanent feature of the political landscape.

The practical effect of all this, of course, has been that in the revenue field, the Commonwealth has established an overlordship. It is quite true that we have made a few relatively minor attempts to give some more flexibility to the States. My own Government went out of the field of entertainment tax and of land tax so that the States might exercise their functions in those fields. There has also occasionally been a proposal that the Commonwealth should go out of the field of collecting death duties, so as to give greater scope for the States in the application of their probate duties. But these are relatively minor items, when compared with direct tax upon incomes about which I have been speaking, and with indirect taxes—excise and customs—which are by Section 90 of the Constitution put within the exclusive jurisdiction of the Commonwealth. Make a note of that, because when I go shopping in a village like New York, I look at the price of something and think 'Yes, I can afford that!' and then find out that to the price is added State and city tax, and what not. In the result, therefore, it must be said that the history of these relations between the Commonwealth and States has, on the revenue side, produced a very great movement in favour of Commonwealth authority.

You will notice that none of this has any relation to a formal amendment of the Constitution. On the contrary, the whole argument over uniform tax, and the whole argument in the two High Court cases in which it was discussed, has made it quite clear that all the things that were done in fact were done under existing Commonwealth power, with no constitutional alteration at all. Now, of course, the revenue side of government is tremendously important, and therefore this was a major revolution without any formal constitutional amendment at all. Another great change had already arisen in relation to the borrowing position of States. It arose because there was a Financial Agreement in 1927 and a constitutional amendment in 1928. About that I will have something to say in another lecture.

7

The Commonwealth-States Financial Agreement and The Operation of the Loan Council

S IR, I'm very glad that you made a very kind introduction, because I was set down originally to do seven lectures; at least there were six when President Shannon invited me very courteously, and for once in his life he had the invitee writing back and saying 'I don't think I can do it in less than seven'. So I got to work on seven and this is number five, and looking over them I want to warn you at once, in case any of you have urgent appointments elsewhere, that this will be the dullest of the lot—because some of the others had a gleam of humanity in them, and this one is all about the financial operations of the Loan Council of Australia, than which nothing less passionate can be imagined. And so, he that hath no stomach to this fight, let him depart!

I have shown, to such of you as have heard my earlier lectures, how, under the initial necessities of war and by an extensive use of the power to make grants under Section 96 of the Australian Constitution, and thereafter by the development of a settled habit of mind on the part of most, if not all of the States, the Commonwealth Parliament has established full control over the raising of income tax; I find this is received with immense pleasure in the corridors of the law faculty. And it has done this without any amendment of the Constitution at all. In short, on the revenue side, the Commonwealth—and mind you, when I speak of the

Commonwealth, I speak of the Commonwealth of Australia, the central organism—already having exclusive recourse to customs and excise under Section 90 of the Constitution (an enormous source of revenue in each case) has now secured, in effect, exclusive recourse to income tax, the other major source of revenue.

Now, Alfred Deakin, one of the founding fathers and subsequently a distinguished Prime Minister of Australia, speaking in 1902, with no reason to anticipate the judicial events of the then distant future, made a prophetic statement. He said then:

> As the power of the purse in Great Britain established by degrees the authority of the Commons, so it will in Australia ultimately establish the authority of the Commonwealth. The rights of self-government of the States have been fondly supposed to be safeguarded by the Constitution. It has left them legally free, but financially bound to the chariot wheels of the Commonwealth.

This forecast will be seen to be doubly true when I turn away from the revenue side, with which I dealt last lecture, to the capital or borrowing side of the picture.

In the 'twenties' Commonwealth and States competed with each other on the loan markets in Australia or abroad. The 'credit ratings' of the various borrowers were not uniform. There arose a growing feeling that this was tending to force up interest rates and have unsatisfactory effects on the loan markets themselves.

Therefore, the Bruce Government, Mr (now Lord) Bruce then being Prime Minister, after some experimental arrangements, proposed to the States that a Financial Agreement should be prepared and executed to regulate and control government borrowing, and that, to ensure its continuing effect, the necessary Constitutional Amendment should be promoted.

It was decided that inducements were to be offered. I would hope that 'inducements' is the right word, but you'll be able to determine that. But they determined that they ought to offer inducements, and I should explain this.

Section 94 of the Constitution provides that: 'After five years from the imposition of uniform duties of customs, the Parliament *may provide*, on such basis as it deems fair, for the monthly payment to the several States of all surplus revenue of the Commonwealth.'

The Commonwealth, though the provisions of Section 94 seemed on the face of them permissive only, avoided all practical risks by enacting the Surplus Revenue Act of 1908, which established the practice of appropriating to Commonwealth 'trust' accounts revenues unexpended at the end of the financial year. This meant that there was no 'surplus' revenue! And the method was upheld in the case of *New South Wales* v. *The Commonwealth* (1908) 7 C.L.R. 179. (I may add that the practice continues in full vigour.) The Bill appropriating to trust accounts (for example, to the Defence fund) is still just about the last Bill in every financial year. Our financial year ends 30 June. On about 29 June, in comes the last Bill, and it appropriates to trust accounts what otherwise might have been surplus revenue. Well, this must have come as a blow to the expectations of the States, whose responsibilities were tending to outstrip their resources. So, in the Prime Ministership of Andrew Fisher, who was the Labour Prime Minister in 1910 and had a fine Scots burr on his tongue—in 1910, a Surplus Revenue Act was passed, providing out of the Commonwealth budget *per capita* payments to the States for ten years. And those payments were continued until 1927. In 1927, under the Bruce Administration, by the States Grants Act of 8 April, 1927, the Commonwealth Parliament repealed the *per capita* payments provisions of the Surplus Revenue Act, as from 30 June, 1927. Now, this may seem a humdrum record to you, but you see the position.

The States were getting a *per capita* payment; they were not getting surplus revenue because there was none by definition or by legislation. But they were getting *per capita* payments. And then the Commonwealth wanted them to make an agreement, so it cut off the *per capita* payments. This is, I think, an admirably effective method of negotiation!

And the States were thus put under great financial pressure to make the Financial Agreement which was then under offer to them.

Section 6 of the States Grants Act of 1927, the one which repealed, posed the problem quite plainly for the States. It said:

> Subject to the terms of any agreement made between the Commonwealth and all the States, and adopted by the Parliament, the Treasurer shall, during the financial year commencing on the 1st of July 1927, make payments to each State, in equal monthly instalments, to the amounts specified in the Schedule.

And the amounts so set out were actually, though not expressly, calculated on the previous *per capita* payments. So you see what this meant. You make an agreement, and you'll continue to get grants based roughly on your *per capita* requirements; you don't make an agreement, and you're standing outside all surplus revenue and all *per capita* payments. Even I could have understood that.

Well, the inducements proved palatable, and the pressure succeeded, and all the States signed on the dotted line.

The terms of the Agreement, the more important of which I'll deal with a little later, contemplated that for full validity a Constitutional Amendment would be required; its terms were set out in Part IV of the Agreement.

The Amendment was (as I said in my first Lecture) submitted to the people and carried, and is now Section 105A of the Constitution. It gives power to the Commonwealth to make agreements with the States with respect to the public debts of the States, including, among other things, 'the borrowing of money by the States or by the Commonwealth, or by the Commonwealth for the States'.

It also provided that 'The Parliament may make laws for the carrying out by the parties thereto of any such agreement'.

Well, there were and there are two other significant provisions. One of them was this:

(4) Any such agreement may be varied or rescinded by the parties thereto.

That is to say, it requires unanimity, and unanimity between each and every State and the Commonwealth is in Australia, in the jargon of the economists, 'in short supply'.

The Financial Agreement Act, 1944, a later one, referred to several agreements made pursuant to Section 105A. I don't need to go into the details, because they made no vital change in principle or structure. They were related to financial procedures which had, in the light of experience, including wartime experience, proved to be reasonably necessary. So far, these have been the only amendments, and a really basic change, having regard to the unanimity requirement, is not to be expected.

As I indicated briefly in my initial lecture, the Government of Victoria, before its Premier signed the Agreement, took counsel's opinion, a very good thing to do. All Governments ought to be encouraged to do this. And I was one of the two counsel engaged to give the opinion. My colleague and I issued, quite in vain, a series of warnings about the probable effects of the Agreement upon the financial independence of the States. This was long before I became immersed in political affairs. In particular, we said, and I'll quote the words, as I looked up the opinion not long ago, that we thought that 'the High Court would be inclined to put a very extended meaning upon the words of the proposed constitutional alteration, and that, if this were so, there would be practically no limits to the extent of interference with the property and activities of the State which might be regarded as coming within the words "carrying out or giving effect to any such agreement" '. We even said, rather daringly, as we thought at the time: 'A law might be made under which a Receiver of State revenue might be put in on behalf of the Commonwealth.'

Well, sir, these remarks turned out to be well-founded, because in 1932, the then Government of New South Wales, of set policy, the great Depression then being current, failed to provide certain interest payments on its public debts in accordance with the Financial Agreement. In blunt, it repudiated them. The then Premier of New South Wales was a man named Lang, and the slogan was painted on every roadway by ardent supporters, and on railroad bridges— later on devoted to abuse of me—'Lang is right; Lang is right; Lang is right'. These words rang around his State, interlarded with 'Greater than Lenin'. Anyhow, he repudiated the interest obligations, and the Commonwealth passed two enforcement Acts which provided for the seeking of a Declaration of the amount payable and unpaid by the State, and went on to provide that the ensuing judgment should operate as a charge upon all the revenue of the State, payments of which were to be made to the Commonwealth. So my learned colleague and I turned out to be right.

And in *New South Wales* v. *Commonwealth* (1931) 46 C.L.R. 155, the High Court upheld the validity of this law. Mr Justice Starke, to whom I made a courteous reference in one or two earlier lectures, took the opportunity of saying:

It has been strenuously asserted that these Acts are an interference with the sovereign rights of the States. . . . But, as has been pointed out more than once in this court, the States are not sovereign powers.

This is a species of blasphemy, I suppose, south of the Mason-Dixon Line, but I still believe it to be true.

The Financial Agreement thus secured, and to which I now return, was signed on 12 December, 1928, and was in due course approved by each of the State Parliaments.

Though the effects of the Agreement have been quite revolutionary in practice, it seems probable that the draftsmen of the Agreement thought they were doing little more than to provide a means to rationalize borrowing arrangements between Commonwealth and State Governments, and thereby to strengthen the credit of those Governments in local and overseas markets.

Still less was it realized by the State Governments that the Agreement could enlarge the supremacy of the Commonwealth over the States. The Premier of Victoria, for example, undeterred by the legal opinion he had received from my learned friend and myself, expressed the view that the Agreement represented a rather good deal for the States, and would tend to even up and stabilize the balance between them and the Commonwealth.

It would be tedious, and unnecessary for my present purpose, to go through the Agreement in detail.

The Commonwealth took over the State public debts. Commonwealth and States were to contribute to the necessary sinking funds. There were provisions about the payment of interest, and the like.

But the major achievement was the creation of the Australian Loan Council, made up of a representative of the Commonwealth—*a* representative of the Commonwealth—and one from each of the six States. I might add as an aside that there are always two representing the Commonwealth, but only one votes. The Treasurer is the Chairman of the Loan Council, and in my time the Prime Minister always sat next to him, and in the most impertinent fashion, took a hand in the argument. But there is one voting representative from the Commonwealth and one from each of the six States.

When a matter comes to issue and has to be voted upon, the Commonwealth has two votes, and the States one each. In addition, the Commonwealth has a casting vote. Now, it follows that the Commonwealth can succeed in any division in which it secures the support of *two* States out of six. Meetings of the Loan Council, normally held once or sometimes twice a year, are convened by the Commonwealth, although three States can, and occasionally do, demand that a meeting be held.

Each year the Council decides on a loan works 'programme', the actual borrowing being made by the Commonwealth. Clause 4 of the agreement provides that—(I am leaving out the irrelevant words):

> the Commonwealth . . . shall . . . arrange for all borrowings for or on behalf of the Commonwealth or any State....

It is worth noting that some unsuccessful attempts have been made, in the interests of the States, to establish the proposition that the Commonwealth's obligation to 'arrange' loans imports an obligation to procure the money. In fact, this argument implied that if the Commonwealth's loan was under-subscribed on the market the Commonwealth should be obliged to make up the short-fall by discounting Treasury Bills with the Central Bank.

This I would be willing to describe as a wrong interpretation of the Agreement. Indeed, it has never been pursued. And indeed it was not until eighteen years after the Financial Agreement that the Commonwealth obtained power to issue directions on policy to the Central Bank; a power which included directions to discount Treasury Bills for loan short-fall purposes.

Then the Agreement provides for the main function to be performed by the Loan Council in these terms:

3 (*g*) The Commonwealth and each State will from time to time . . . submit to the Loan Council a programme setting forth the amount it desires to raise by loans for each financial year for purposes other than the conversion renewal or redemption of existing loans or loans for temporary purposes. Each programme shall state the estimated total amount of such loan expenditure for the year, and the estimated amount of repayments which will be available towards meeting it. Any revenue deficit to be funded shall be included in such loan programme. Loans for defence purposes approved by the Parliament of the Commonwealth shall not be included in the Commonwealth's loan programme or be otherwise subject to this Agreement.

And then, again:

3 (*h*) If the Loan Council decides that the total amount of the loan programme for the year [don't forget, the loan programme is the one that is hammered out when the Loan Council meets] cannot be borrowed at reasonable rates and conditions it shall decide the amount to be borrowed for the year, and may by unanimous decision allocate such amount between the Commonwealth and the States.

Well, one of the reasons, or the main reason why I am considering this aspect of financial control after my examination of uniform tax, although this came later on, is that, though uniform taxation came many years after the Financial Agreement, it is to the operation of that Agreement, and particularly the work of the Loan Council, *since the last war*, that particular significance attaches.

Now, sir, I first watched the operations of the Loan Council in Canberra in the years before the war, from 1935 on.

The demands upon the loan market were very small, compared with the demands during and after the war.

The Loan Council at that time really believed that its function was to decide, and indeed the contract said so, what amount of the projected loan programme could be borrowed 'at reasonable rates and conditions', and that the amount so determined would be the amount to be borrowed. It had, of course, the advice of loan market experts; but, more importantly, it had the Banks, through the Commonwealth Bank, now called the Reserve Bank—the Government Bank —as the underwriters of the loans. I have very vivid and whimsical memories of what went on. The members of the Loan Council (it was only thirty years ago) would propose an amount; it was usually £25 million or something like that. It's hard to imagine it today. The Commonwealth representative would pronounce an interval and go out and have a conference with the representatives of the Bank and would come back with, usually, a modified proposal. It was down from twenty-five to twenty-one, let's say. By the end of the day, with a few of these intervals and a little communion of souls between the Treasurer of the Commonwealth and the Commonwealth Bank and the Premiers, agreement was reached. It probably ended up being at twenty-two and one half or something like that. The market prospects became irrelevant because the loan was underwritten. All that remained then was, by unanimous decision, to 'cut up the turkey', to use the picturesque metaphor of one of the Premiers, and to go home.

See, there it was—reasonable rates and conditions, the loan programme established. The loans would be issued by the Commonwealth, they would all be underwritten, and then we took the twenty-two and one-half million that I mentioned out, and said how much each State should get, and then of course the second argument began.

Well, the war period was, of course, one in which the

primacy of Commonwealth war loans was undisputed. With the outbreak of war, the vast unemployment of the Depression years—which in fact was thirty per cent at its peak in 1932, in the time of Mr Lang—gave way to labour shortages. All possible resources had to be moved over to fill war requirements. The defence needs, including recourse to the loan market, were accepted as paramount. The States' demands clearly had to be reduced to a minimum; the State Governments patriotically and readily agreed to this. So, in a sense, the Loan Council's functions were limited.

However, during my own first Prime Ministership, in 1940, the Loan Council, in order to secure 'co-ordinated action by the Commonwealth and States to secure the maximum defence effort', appointed a Co-ordinator of Works, with whom there should act a Works Officer appointed by each State. And the Loan Council Co-ordinator was to submit to the Loan Council recommendations for State borrowings for civil purposes including deficits, with all necessary practical details. Well, the appointments were made, but as the war effort grew, the claims of State works were reduced inevitably to small proportions. As a shrewd commentator put it to me, the instrument for co-ordination had been created, but it had little to co-ordinate.

In the result, as you will realize, the Loan Council during the war became in a practical sense an agent of Commonwealth policy, directing itself to the common task of concentrating resources on the national effort. This strengthened the idea that the Loan Council, with the special position and power which the Commonwealth held in it, could become a focal point in national public investment planning.

After the War, a new practice arose, which reached its greatest strength under my own second Government. It is of that period that I can speak particularly with first-hand knowledge.

Every State found itself with new and enormous demands for public works and housing—both largely and inevitably deferred during the War—schools and hospitals, roads, water-supply for developing rural industries, and a host of other matters, which were the inevitable back-log of a long period of wartime restrictions and self-denials.

Well, the loan programmes presented by the States, programmes which were vetted (for capacity to perform) by the Co-ordinator-General, reached totals which were far beyond any realistic loan market estimate. And the Commonwealth Bank and the Banks were no longer willing to be the underwriters.

So, nominally under the Financial Agreement, a new practice came to be adopted which, in my opinion, departed from the terms of the Agreement, but achieved a not unsatisfactory result. In form, the Agreement was not amended; by common consent, it was ignored. Of such stuff, sir, are revolutionary constitutional changes made.

Now what happened was this. Even after heavy pruning, year after year it was quite clear to all at the Loan Council table that the total amount required could not reasonably be borrowed on the market. So we would have a process of bargaining, at the end of which the Commonwealth would say (I just take figures at random) 'Our estimate of the Loan Market is 150 million pounds. We think that the reasonable total *requirement* of the States is £200 million. We won't take any share of the market for ourselves.' We began in this way. 'We won't actually underwrite loans of £200 million, we'll be prepared to advance monthly for six months to the States on the basis of a year's total of £200 million. At the end of the first half of the year, with more experience of the market, we will have another look at the position.'

Well, in effect, year after year, the States went home outwardly protesting but sometimes, not always, inwardly content, and, as the monthly payments always ran on through the full year, the Commonwealth found itself supplementing the market yield by massive subventions out of its Budget. As we couldn't get it from the market, we had to get it from somewhere—keeping taxes up in consequence, and not infrequently, as I remember with a grim smile, being abused about the taxation level by some of the beneficiaries. This is a phenomenon with which you are very familiar, or will be. In most years in my time as Prime Minister, the Loan Council has not purported to decide how much could be borrowed 'at reasonable rates and conditions'. It has fixed a loan works programme which the Commonwealth has been willing to accept, and has distributed it, by agreement, among the States. This new procedure, adopted by tacit consent without any formal amendment of the Financial Agreement has, as you won't have failed to notice, given the Commonwealth effective overall control of the States' works programmes. It may be interesting to record how this new practice arose.

In 1950 there was a war in Korea and there was a great boom in raw materials, a boom very powerfully contributed to by some singularly incompetent wool buying on behalf of the United States of America. I don't want to go into that in detail, but it is true. And the price of wool went up to the sky. Well, wool is the greatest source of export income in Australia, and there was already some inflation caused by shortages of labour; the wool boom created a tremendous inflationary pressure. In the result, works projects were held up, retail prices were at one stage rising at the rate of twenty-five per cent per annum. Our overseas reserves ran down rapidly. And for these and other reasons, the loan market was very sick.

My own Government's Budget for 1951–2 was extremely drastic, and included heavy increases in taxation to produce a counter-inflationary budget surplus.

In the same financial year, the States' programmes submitted to the Loan Council totalled £300 million as compared with a gross loan expenditure of £167 million in the previous year. That's roughly twice as much. Two facts were clearly established. The loan market would not supply more than a fraction of what was needed. The loan market is always unhealthy when you have inflationary conditions, of course. Large sums of money over and above the estimated market yield must be found if the States were not to close down many projects and in some cases actually default on current contracts for works and supplies.

Now, five States out of six could, by their majority in the Loan Council, have approved their full programme; one or two States in fact wanted to do so. But any such approval would have been quite futile if (as was correctly assumed) the money would not be normally borrowed and the Commonwealth was unwilling to provide it from other sources, namely, taxation or the Central Bank.

Well, it was at this stage that my own Commonwealth Government took an unprecedented step. We offered, subject to conditions, to underwrite a borrowing programme. One condition was that the submitted programme should be reduced by a quarter of what they were asking for, from £300 million to £225 million. Another was that State semi-governmental programmes, because there were a lot of semi-governmental programmes; public trusts, etc. with borrowing power;—should be reduced. And our offer was accepted. By similar processes, in the following year, the States' programmes were cut back to £180 million.

I have earlier referred to the cost to the Commonwealth of its support for approved programmes. I think I should explain how we met this cost. It was, from our point of view, important that our payments to the States by way of supplement to the loan market yield should be repayable. If they were made by way of grant, unrepayable grant, there would be no inducement to the States to assist in making the loans issued on the market a success, and that assistance was vital to the success of those loans.

Now, under Clause 4 (4) of the Financial Agreement, 'money shall not be borrowed by the Commonwealth or any State otherwise than in accordance with this Agreement.'

How, then, could the Commonwealth make a loan to a State, a loan which would not have its origin in the Financial Agreement or in the Loan Council, but arise outside its terms?

Well, the difficulty was surmounted in this way. The Commonwealth Treasurer had power under the Audit Act to invest the Trust Fund. (You will remember I spoke earlier about the creation of the Trust Fund as a means of avoiding surplus revenue, tucking it away if I may say so.) If actual borrowings fell short of the Loan Council programme, as they chronically did by, say, £60 million, there would be an appropriation of £60 million from the Commonwealth's Consolidated Revenue to an account forming part of the Trust Fund, called the Loan Consolidation and Investment Reserve. And then the Commonwealth would arrange with the States for the floating of an internal loan of £60 million. The Fund, the Trust Fund, the Loan Consolidation and Investment Reserve, would then subscribe the £60 million to the loan. Everybody was, to use a grossly inaccurate phrase, happy. The States got the full amount of cash specified in the approved programme, and the Commonwealth got the necessary interest-bearing securities.

This process clearly extends the Commonwealth ascendancy over the States, for it enables the Commonwealth to decide from year to year what the level of State loan works will be, and to have a great influence upon the level of semi-governmental loan works also.

Decisions taken by the Loan Council are still, of course, expressed in financial terms. Respect is thus paid to the Financial Agreement. But the procedure adopted is of relevance to my thesis. The States submit programmes which are normally much larger than could physically be carried out in the financial year, and they know it. The Loan Council endorses this as 'Works programmes', and then, 'persuaded' by the Commonwealth, 'approves' a lesser amount as a borrowing programme.

In short, the Loan Council tends to become a central piece of machinery in an economic planning concept involving Commonwealth and States' co-operation.

Now, the importance of all that will be at once seen.

Yet though what I have said shows a new form of power, the Commonwealth has so far stopped short of trying to prescribe the purposes for which the States may spend the money thus obtained. In other words, there are no strings on it. There are, in my opinion, two reasons for this abstention, one theoretical, and one very practical.

The theoretical reason is that, as good Federalists, we would not wish to impair the autonomy of the States in the important functions for which they are responsible. Clearly the strictness with which this principle is applied will depend very much on political circumstances and contemporary pressures.

But the practical reason is that the Commonwealth knows that the States are better informed and better equipped administratively and technically in relation to their constitutional functions, their 'reserved' or 'residuary' powers, and that overall efficiency would suffer from too large a Commonwealth invasion.

Now, in my own time as Prime Minister this new practice that I have been describing of making subventions to pick up the loan market short-fall, and to see that the loan works programme goes through; this new practice has involved the most extensive financial subventions by the Commonwealth.

I will express the amount of Commonwealth assistance to

the agreed Loan Council Works and Housing programme, that is, assistance to supplement the loan yield, as a percentage of the total.

In 1951–2, the year I mentioned when we had this terrific boom of inflation, it was no less than 67 per cent of the total.

In 1952–3, it was 69 per cent of the total.

Over the next five years, it tapered off a bit: it averaged 40 per cent of the total.

And in the following seven years the loan market having improved, the subvention fell, on the average of those seven years, to about 11 per cent of the total.

But if you look over the whole period of sixteen years of my own administration, the average was 28 per cent of the total. In other words, 28 per cent of the whole loan works programmes of the States for all purposes came out of Commonwealth provision and not from the loan market.

All this departure from the strict letter of the Financial Agreement has been well warranted by the developmental needs of the nation. It has enabled the States to maintain a large volume of public works. But it has emphasized the dependence of the States on the Commonwealth and, because each year the Commonwealth Government has acted without technical obligation—let me remind you of that; this has all been without technical obligation—and has therefore exercised its own discretion as a Commonwealth Government; it has strengthened, *de facto*, the financial authority of the Commonwealth.

Now, Commonwealth Governments have, I believe, so far observed a decent moderation in the use of this power. But as demands for financial assistance grow, and as the habit of looking to Canberra for all good things persists, the day may come when, at a Loan Council meeting, a Commonwealth Government will say: 'Well, the price you are to pay for our budgetary assistance to the loan programme is that we must approve of the items in your works programme.' And under such circumstances a State, or States, could in theory reply by saying: 'Well, let's go back to the Financial Agreement, and perform the functions of the Loan Council strictly according to the Agreement terms.' But this, of course, would be the straight road to State bankruptcy. It would leave them in a hopeless financial position.

To sum up, it is very small wonder that Mr Justice Dixon in the *Melbourne Corporation Case* said, with his usual restraint:

> The Financial Agreement under Section 105A of the Constitution and the adoption of the system of uniform taxation placed the finances of the States in a very different position from that which they occupied when the Commonwealth was first established.

Now, there is one other point which perhaps I should briefly discuss. You may well ask what happens if the States cannot agree about the allocation of the agreed total amount of the programme. The answer is that in that event, which for a variety of reasons has not yet occurred, the 'formula' would apply. The formula, the blessed word 'formula'.

Well, the Financial Agreement provides for it in these terms. I want you to listen to this very very carefully because some of the cleverer of you may be able to explain to me later on what it means; I'll read it to you:

> If the members of the Loan Council fail to arrive at a unanimous decision under the last preceding sub-clause allocating the amount to be borrowed for any year, the amount to be borrowed for that year shall be allocated as follows:
>
> (1) The Commonwealth shall, if it so desires, be entitled to have one-fifth or any less proportion of such amount allocated to the Commonwealth; and
> (2) Each State shall be entitled to have allocated to it a sum (being a portion of the balance of such amount)

bearing to the balance of such amount the same proportion which the net loan expenditure of that State in the preceding five years bears to the net loan expenditure of all the States during the same period.

And there follows a proviso which, fortunately, is immaterial to my present purpose.

Well, this formula, as you will see, ladies and gentlemen, at a glance; you know, just taking a swift look at it, this formula was weighted in favour of the States who had been the largest borrowers. And it was and is therefore not uniformly popular at the Loan Council table. And there have been, I think, three reasons for this, each depending on modern practice.

First, the Commonwealth has now for many years not claimed its one-fifth, but left the total to the States, carrying its own works programme on revenue, much to the dissatisfaction of financial and economic purists, but much to the benefit of the States. For reasons of sheer arithmetic, the Commonwealth could, if it wanted to, frustrate an appeal to the formula by saying that it would insist on its own one-fifth itself and the States would be worse off.

Second, in strict theory, the Commonwealth could, in the majority of recent years, exercise discipline by refusing to supplement the proceeds of the loan market; a refusal which as I have pointed out would in most years of my own Prime Ministership have seriously reduced the amount to be allocated. This, of course, would be drastic, and in most if not all cases opposed to the overall interest. But the possibility remains in the unspoken background, and adds to the influence of the Commonwealth. I beg of all you students to remember that the background is not always noisy; it's when the background is unspoken that it tends to be most powerful.

Third, the differences are usually adjusted by informal

meetings of Treasury officials who advise their Ministers. And these gentlemen are, in my experience, extremely able, and not subject to, or much influenced by, political storms. They talk a lot of good sense to their ministerial heads. Occasionally some relatively small adjustment is made either by some State conceding something, which is a rare but honourable event, or by some supplementary provision by the Commonwealth—which of course we always made with a high gesture, as long as it did not cost too much.

After all, at a Loan Council meeting, each Premier knows that he may want some help himself at some future time, and he should not make enemies lightly. And in the result, the formula has not been applied.

On no occasion that is recorded did a State Premier actually demand the application of the 'formula', though I can remember several occasions on which some Premier made pointed reference to his 'formula position' or his 'rights under the formula'. They always stopped short.

The truth is that the formula, as I hinted to you earlier, in my usual delicacy, is somewhat ambiguously worded, so that nobody can say with confidence what it means. There have been many discussions without agreement on interpretation, but there has been no recourse to the Courts.

You will have appreciated that though the Financial Agreement and its sequels have brought about an enhancement of Commonwealth power, there have developed some disadvantages in a system which produces a certain amount of rigidity in the sharing-out of the loan programmes between the States. For, even in the absence of any strict application of the distribution formula, practice had induced a measure of uniformity from one year to another.

Well, sir, I must confess that, for a highly individualistic people, we have in the Australian Constitution and have had in our organized political thinking a strange passion for uniformity, and in particular the avoidance of discrimination between States. Yet Australia is not a uniform country, and the problems of the States are not uniform. Our resources and our developmental needs vary greatly from one State to another. It is this fact which has brought Section 96, about which I was speaking a fortnight ago, and the modern use of Commonwealth grants to the States into play as, to some extent, a corrective.

Now another compensating factor has been that setting up of semi-governmental authorities to take care of major undertakings in power, water supply, sewerage, ports, and the like, to which I made some reference earlier. And here, as I illustrated in another connection in an earlier lecture, there can be detected two currents of opinion which are in some philosophical conflict. In the field of education, for example, there is constant pressure to make the Commonwealth accept comprehensive responsibilities. I have always resisted this myself, on the ground that centralized national responsibility and authority in education would tend to produce uniformity. And I put my view on this matter in a speech to the Australian College of Education in May of 1961, in these words, and as I have some noted educationalists in my audience, I will quote what I then said:

It's just because I think that too much uniformity in education is bad, and philosophically considered, self-defeating, that I don't believe that the constitutional power over education should be transferred to the Commonwealth Parliament. In a continent like ours, with immense varieties of physical and human characteristics, variety should be developed. Men are different. It is just because they are different that our parliamentary democracy survives. For the greatest of all liberties is that which exists in a man's own mind. It is a liberty of which he alone is master, and it makes him to that extent a master, not a servant. Produce in a nation a generation of men and women with liberty in their own individual minds, and dictatorship becomes impossible.

Montesquieu, who has had such an influence upon organic political science, had no respect for uniformity. He looked for a system of government (which the United States and Australia to a degree adopted) where there is a division of power, where power checks power. He firmly believed, and I quote his words, 'that the idea of uniformity appealed to little minds, who found in it a species of perfection'.

But the pressure goes on.

And I take another example. There is widespread political and public interest in the Northern Development of Australia; a development which can only be fully achieved by differential treatment of differing areas with differing resources. I have earlier referred to Section 99 of our Constitution, forbidding the giving of preference in any revenue law 'to one State or any part thereof over another State or any part thereof'.

Well, to encourage settlement in the Northern and tropical areas, Parliament splendidly ignored this provision by enacting special tax provisions relating to parts of States in these areas; Zone A and Zone B. And so far although one man thought of it until he was thrown out on another point, its validity has not been effectively challenged. Well, these provisions are widely approved, because in dealing with this problem of development, the disabilities of uniformity are clearly and publicly perceived.

And so, sir, as I said to you earlier, it may well turn out that the flexible use of Section 96 grants will modify in practice the austerities of Section 99.

8

The External Affairs Power of the Commonwealth

THOSE of you who have survived so far will know that I have been talking about a broad theme, which is how the powers of the central Government in the Australian Federation have grown, principally by means other than formal amendment. Tonight I want to say to you that the Commonwealth's 'external affairs' power—because that is how it is expressed in the Commonwealth Constitution —affords another striking example of how in the process of interpretation, powers may assume a new appearance.

Now, under Section 51 (xxix) of the Commonwealth Constitution, the Commonwealth Parliament has power to make laws for the peace, order and good government of the Commonwealth with respect to 'External Affairs'. That is the simple phrase. Section 51 (xxix) adds—'Matters incidental to the execution of any power vested by this Constitution in the Parliament . . .'.

In the United States your Constitution declares that the President shall have power to make treaties and also provides that, and I quote the words—'this Constitution, and the laws of the United States . . . made in pursuance thereof; and all treaties made . . . under the authority of the United States shall be the supreme law of the land'. You see how different it is.

No such pre-eminence was expressly given to treaties by the Australian Constitution. Incidentally, though this is of no moment, though no great point is to be made about it, the power over external affairs in our Constitution comes twenty-ninth in a list of forty enumerated powers contained in Section 51.

And the modest placing of the power is not to be wondered at. When the Australian Constitution was being fashioned, the Empire—the British Empire—still existed and its foreign policies were controlled from Whitehall. Australia was not confronted by any external threat, and most of her people had little interest in the international political affairs of the world. For many years, although there was always, I am happy to say, a Minister for External Affairs, who usually had another portfolio, there was no real Department of External Affairs. It was not until the late thirties that Australia began to expand her overseas representation.

A High Commissionership to the United Kingdom was created by an Act of 1909. In my first term as Prime Minister, which began in 1939, we appointed the first High Commissioner to Canada, and opened legations in Washington and Tokyo. Today we have diplomatic posts all round the world, and a large, active, and highly-trained Department.

I mention these facts to establish, if I need to, that when the draftsmen of the Constitution wrote down the magic words 'external affairs', there did not leap into their minds any vision of the complex and novel things that were to come many years later. Least of all could they have imagined a comprehensive world organization of which Australia would be a member, that there would be an International Labour Organization, or that the political stuff of nineteenth-century treaties would largely have substituted for it the bargaining of merchants, of exporters and importers, agreements in the fields of health and science, the literally hundreds of matters engaging our attention and turning our eyes out to other lands and other peoples.

External affairs, once a matter of almost trifling substance, has become, with Prime Minister's, Treasury, and Trade, one of the four most significant Departments of State.

Now, sir, what are 'external affairs'? Most of the other powers (not all, as I pointed out in the case of the defence power) relate to concrete, identifiable subject matters. The external affairs power is in vague terms, and its scope is not defined. Here, indeed, is a fertile field for the labours of the judicial interpreter.

As in other instances, the narrow or limited view appears to have been the received view in the earlier years of the new nation. Thus, the late Professor Sir William Harrison Moore, a great legal scholar under whom I studied at the Melbourne University, and whose memory I revere, in his *Commonwealth of Australia*, 2nd Edition, 1910, wrote this:

> The power to give effect to international arrangements must, it would seem, be limited to matters which *in se* concern external relations; a matter in itself purely domestic, and therefore within the exclusive power of the States, can't be drawn within the range of federal power merely because some arrangement has been made for uniform national action. Thus, there is at the present time an international movement for the amelioration of labour conditions, and the International Union has arrived at some agreements for uniformity of legislation. It is submitted that the Commonwealth could not by adhering to an international agreement for the regulation of factories and workshops, proceed to legislate upon that subject in supersession of the laws of the States.

These words were, of course, written before the decision in the *Engineers' Case*, about which I spoke earlier, at a time when the doctrine of the mutual immunity of Commonwealth and State instrumentalities was fully accepted, and when it was thought necessary to construe Commonwealth powers in the light of and in a real sense subject to the 'implied', 'reserved', or 'residuary' powers of the States.

One can also question the proposition that domestic matters are within the 'exclusive power of the States'.

But, as we have seen, the High Court, from 1920 onwards, adopted a broad method of interpretation, applying legal principles of course, but applying them flexibly in the light of changing circumstances.

Now, sir, though there had been several observations on the 'external affairs' power by individual judges, it was many years before the Full High Court found occasion for an elaborate examination of the external affairs power. This was in the case of *The King* v. *Burgess, ex parte Henry* (1936), 55 C.L.R. 608. For my present purpose, the head-note in the report adequately explains the facts:

Section 4 of the Air Navigation Act 1920 authorized the Governor-General to make regulations for the purpose of carrying out and giving effect to the convention for the regulation of aerial navigation signed in Paris on the 13th October 1919, and any amendment thereof, and for the purpose of providing for the control of air navigation in the Commonwealth and the Territories. The convention was made between heads of States of the allied and associated Powers, including the Commonwealth of Australia, and was ratified by his Majesty, King George V, on behalf of the British Empire, on 1st June 1922.

HELD: (by the court)

(1) that so much of Section 4 of the Air Navigation Act 1920 as empowered the Governor-General to make regulations for carrying out and giving effect to the convention was a valid exercise of the 'external affairs' power conferred upon the Commonwealth by Section 51 (xxix) of the Constitution.

It is true that the majority of the Judges went on to find that the Regulations made under the Act departed materially from the Convention and, there being no general power in the Commonwealth to control civil aviation in Australia, invalidity resulted. But the great interest of the case attaches to the interpretation of 'external affairs'.

Well, the Chief Justice in this great case, Chief Justice Latham, thought that the power over 'external affairs' at least included a power to legislate to give effect to the international convention for air navigation. He approached the general problem with some caution. He said, at page 640:

Then, it is argued that the power to legislate with regard to external affairs is limited to matters which *in se* concern external relations or to matters which may properly be the subject matter of international agreement. No criterion has been suggested which can result in designating certain matters as *in se* concerning external relations and excluding all other matters from such a class. It is very difficult to say that any matter is incapable of affecting international relations so as properly to become the subject matter of an international agreement. It appears to me that no absolute rule can be laid down upon this subject. No one would today be inclined to deny that the production and sale of recently invented narcotic drugs is a matter of international interest and concern. Fifty years ago it is unlikely that many persons would have thought that such subjects would be dealt with by international treaties.

Modern invention has almost abolished the effects of distance in time and space which enabled most States to be indifferent to what happened elsewhere. Today all people are neighbours, whether they like it or not, and the endeavour to discover means of living together upon practicable terms—or at least to minimize quarrels—has greatly increased the number of subjects to be dealt with, in some measure, by international action.

And he then went on:

The Department of External Affairs of the Commonwealth published on 15th August 1935 a 'List of International Agreements to which Australia is a party, or which affect Australia, together with prefatory notes'. The list of bilateral international agreements extends over eighteen pages and the list of general and multilateral international agreements extends over eleven pages. The subjects are so various that it is impossible to classify them. They include matters affecting extradition, trade and commerce, navigation, legal proceedings, joint stock companies, war graves, commercial arbitration, international arbitration, tariffs, trade marks and other industrial property, friendship and amity, postal matters, medical practitioners, lunatics, submarine telegraph cables, maritime and land warfare, sanitation, white slave traffic, use of white phosphorus in manufacturing matches, copyright, obscene publications, peace after the Great War, labour matters, contagious diseases, dangerous drugs, economic statistics [I like this; I think Sir John Latham was so right to put economic statistics and dangerous drugs next to each other in this list!] limitation and reduction of armaments, and other subjects. It will be seen therefore that the possible subjects of international agreement are infinitely various. It is in my opinion (and this is the operative part of this judgment)—*It is in my opinion, impossible to say* a priori *that any subject is necessarily such that it could never properly be dealt with by international agreement.* (The italics are mine.)

He went on to emphasize the fact that the power to legislate with respect to external affairs is a power expressly conferred upon the Commonwealth Parliament by the Constitution. 'No question of interference with the rights of the States arises. The Commonwealth Parliament constitutionally possesses the power to legislate as it thinks proper with regard to external affairs, and if any State legislation is inconsistent with Federal legislation on this subject, the State legislation is to the extent of the inconsistency invalid under Section 109 of the Constitution.'

Mr Justice Starke, a fine common lawyer, who was not addicted to general propositions which he thought unnecessary to the decision of the case before him, made three points.

The first one was that the external affairs power must be exercised with regard to the constitutional limitations expressed or implied in the Constitution, namely Sections 92, 113, 116. The Commonwealth cannot do what the Constitution forbids. Well, he was here referring to express provisions such as those in Section 92 (Freedom of Interstate Trade) Section 113 (intoxicating liquids) and Section 116 (against laws for establishing a religion).

His second point was that subject to these limits 'the power is comprehensive in terms and must be commensurate with the obligations that the Commonwealth may properly assume in its relation with other powers or States'. And he, Mr Justice Starke, was disposed to favour an observation by Willoughby, 2nd Edition, that laws will be within the United States treaty making power 'only if the matter is of sufficient international significance to make it a legitimate subject for international co-operation and agreement'.

I merely pause to say that the use of the word 'legitimate' seems to me to leave the most important question unanswered.

And third, Mr Justice Starke, dealing with the air convention said, 'a law providing for the carrying out and giving effect to an international convention of this character concerns

Australia's relations and intercourse with other powers and States and the rights and obligations which result, and is therefore a law for the peace, order and good government of the Commonwealth with respect to external affairs'.

You have heard me, ladies and gentlemen, more than once in the course of these lectures, make proper reference to Mr Justice Dixon, a very great lawyer and man. He made a cautious approach. He said (at p. 669):

> I think it is evident that the purpose of the power was to authorize the Parliament to make laws governing the conduct of Australians in and perhaps out of the Commonwealth in reference to matters affecting the external relations of the Commonwealth . . . some matter indisputably international in character, a law might be made to secure observance of its obligations if they were of a nature affecting the conduct of Australian citizens. On the other hand, it seems an extreme view that merely because the Executive Government undertakes with some other country that the conduct of persons in Australia shall be regulated in a particular way, the legislature thereby obtains a power to enact that regulation although it relates to a matter of internal concern which, apart from the obligation undertaken by the Executive, could not be considered as a matter of external affairs. The limits of the power can only be ascertained authoritatively by a course of decision in which the application of general statements is illustrated by example.

And then, on the other hand, a very broad view was expressed by Mr Justice Evatt and Mr Justice McTiernan. And as this is a view which may well secure more and more supporters as time goes on and as the centripetal forces I have been discussing in these lectures become more powerful, I would like to quote two passages from the Evatt and McTiernan judgment. The first is at p. 687:

It would seem clear, therefore, that the legislative power of the Commonwealth over 'external affairs' certainly includes the power to execute within the Commonwealth treaties and conventions entered into with foreign powers. The legislative power in Section 51 is granted 'subject to this Constitution' so that such treaties and conventions could not be used to enable the Parliament to set at nought constitutional guarantees such, for example, as Sections 6, 28, 41, 80, 92, 99, 100, 116, or 117. But it is not to be assumed that the legislative power over 'external affairs' is limited to the execution of treaties or conventions; and, to pursue the illustration previously referred to, the Parliament may well be deemed competent to legislate for the carrying out of 'recommendations' as well as the 'draft international conventions' resolved upon by the International Labour Organization or of other international recommendations or requests upon other subject matters of concern to Australia as a member of the family of nations. The power is a great and important one.'

If I may interrupt these learned judges, I must say, by way of personal inclination, that the idea that the Commonwealth should apply this power over external affairs to 'recommendations' or 'requests' fills me with apprehension and almost horror about the future of the demarcation of powers.

And then later on, the same two learned judges, having cast an unfavourable verbal glance at my own Government's refusal to ratify the draft conventions of the International Labour Office, a refusal made on the ground that, except for the Conciliation and Arbitration power in Section 51 (xxxv) industrial labour matters were of State jurisdiction, went on to say:

The Commonwealth has power both to enter into international agreements and to pass legislation to secure the carrying out of such agreements according to their tenure even although the subject matter of the agreement is not otherwise within Commonwealth legislative jurisdiction.

The subject matters of these agreements may properly include such matters as, for example, suppression of traffic in drugs, control of armament, regulation of labour conditions and control of air navigation.

It is an essential condition of the power to carry out such international agreements that the local legislation should be in conformity with the terms of the agreement.

And the same two Judges had said earlier (p. 680):

Accordingly, it is wrong to prejudice the examination of the content of the subject 'external affairs' by assuming or asserting *in advance* that there are certain matters such as conditions and terms of employment which are necessarily excluded from Commonwealth legislation in exercise of the power.

We thus see revealed a conflict between two views at least. The *Evatt-McTiernan* view sets no discernible limits to the matters on which the Commonwealth can make international engagements and achieve legislative power to make them effective. It is this view which Dixon described, in the passage I have cited, as an 'extreme view'.

It is worth noting that in the later case of *Ffrost* v. *Stevenson* (1937), 58 C.L.R. at p. 528 this problem was discussed in relation to a quite different matter.

The immediate question was whether the Commonwealth Parliament has power to make legislative provision for the mutual surrender of fugitives between the Mandated Territory of New Guinea and the Commonwealth. For my present purpose, the interest of the case derives from its judicial discussion of the source of power. Chief Justice Latham thought the source was partly Section 122, and partly Section 51 (xxix) 'external affairs'. Section 122 was and is:

> The Parliament may make laws for the Government of any territory surrendered by any State to and accepted by the Commonwealth, or of any territory placed by the Queen under the authority of and accepted by the Commonwealth, or otherwise acquired by the Commonwealth, and may allow the representation of such territory in either House of the Parliament to the extent and on the terms which it thinks fit.

Now, I say nothing about the fascinating problem, much discussed before and by the judges, of whether the 'Mandated Territory of New Guinea' came within this power. My present task is to expound the 'external affairs' power. Now again Chief Justice Latham said at p. 557:

> New Guinea is a place which is outside of His Majesty's dominions and, though it is a territory under the authority of the Commonwealth, it is not itself a part of the Commonwealth, though the Commonwealth is authorized to govern New Guinea as an integral portion of the Commonwealth. Thus the relations between New Guinea and the Commonwealth form part of the subject of external affairs. Provisions for reciprocal surrender of persons charged with criminal offences constitute one of the most ordinary forms of legislation with respect to external affairs. Therefore, under Section 51 (xxxix) of the Constitution, the Commonwealth Parliament has power to legislate for the peace, order and good government of the Commonwealth with respect to the surrender by the Commonwealth to New Guinea and the acceptance in the Commonwealth from New Guinea of such persons. . . .

Mr Justice Evatt once more went into action, basing his views entirely upon the external affairs power. He said:

Section 51 (xxix) and not Section 122 is the source of the Commonwealth's *legislative* power to govern New Guinea in pursuance of the *executive* power and international duty to carry out the obligations imposed on it by the terms of the Mandate.

And later on, the same learned judge said at pages 596–7,

In the *King* v. *Burgess*, *McTiernan J.* and I expressed our definite opinion that, in pursuance of its powers to legislate in respect of 'external affairs', the Commonwealth Parliament is endowed with authority to pass laws giving effect to treaties and conventions without reference to the State Parliaments, provided that such Commonwealth laws are made for the purpose of carrying out the terms of the International Treaty or Convention which has been ratified by the Commonwealth Executive. The question being one of fundamental principle, we stated our views elaborately, holding that if power exists to carry out the Air Convention it exists equally to carry out the International Labour Conventions made within the framework of the I.L.O. Chief Justice Latham gave an impressive list of subjects—including labour matters—as to which the Commonwealth had become a party to conventions and treaties, and in relation to all of which the Commonwealth Parliament had undoubted power to pass legislation which will effectively carry into law throughout Australia the terms of the Conventions. . . .

I make this citation, but it needs a gloss. Chief Justice Latham, as I have indicated, certainly did set out, on the records of the Department of External Affairs, a long list of conventions and treaties affecting Australia, but he did not (as I understand his judgment) commit himself to the proposition that in the case of ALL of them Commonwealth legislative power would exist. What Chief Justice Latham did, as I have pointed out, was to say that *a priori* it could not be said that a subject is *necessarily* excluded from the power.

Mr Justice Evatt then discussed the Canadian power in Section 132 of the Canadian Constitution, the British North America Act of 1867, about which the Chief Justice had said in the *Burgess* case (*supra*, at p. 643) 'The Government and Parliament of the Commonwealth have, in relation to Australia, the powers mentioned in Section 132 of the British North America Act 1867'.

Well, I pause to say, of course, that Chief Justice Latham did not say this as a complete definition of the Commonwealth power.

Section 132 of the British North America Act 1867 reads:

> The Parliament and Government of Canada shall have all powers necessary or proper for performing the obligations of Canada or of any province thereof, as part of the British Empire towards foreign countries, arising under treaties between the Empire and such foreign countries.

Mr Justice Evatt pointed out that this power was much narrower than the 'external affairs' power in Australia. He said, in *Ffrost* v. *Stevenson* at pp. 597–8:

> In its recent decision *A.G. for Canada* v. *A.G. for Ontario*, 1937 A.C. 325, the Privy Council denied the right of the Parliament of the Dominion of Canada to pass laws for the purpose of carrying out certain international labour conventions throughout Canada unless the subject matter of the conventions was otherwise within the competence of the Dominion Parliament as a subject already specified in Section 91 of the Canadian Constitution. But it is necessary to understand the method by which the court reached this conclusion. Under the Canadian Constitution, the subject of legislating for the

performance of treaty obligations is dealt with by a special section, 132, which is entirely separate from Section 91, dealing with the general powers of the Dominion Parliament. By the very terms of Section 132 the power of the Dominion Parliament to legislate for the carrying out of treaty obligations is confined to those obligations which bind Canada as a part of the British Empire. It does not extend to the obligations of Canada entered into upon its own international responsibility. The Privy Council held that the obligations entered into by the Dominion of Canada to carry out certain of the Labour Conventions, although they were internationally binding on Canada, were 'not obligations of Canada as part of the British Empire, but of Canada, by virtue of her new status as an international person . . . and do not arise under a treaty between the British Empire and foreign countries'.

And so, finally, Mr Justice Evatt said at p. 599:

. . . But, unlike Section 132 of the Canadian Constitution, Section 51 (xxix) cannot be limited to treaties entered into by Australia as part of the Empire and necessarily extends to all treaties and conventions entered into by Australia 'by virtue of her new status as an international person' or otherwise. In the case of the Commonwealth treaty obligations, the variety, both as to subject matter and of form of adherence is illustrated by the documents quoted by Chief Justice Latham in R. v. *Burgess*. It is obvious that, if Australia has power to give effect to any of the obligations *bona fide* entered into as an international person, she has power to give effect to them all.

Well, sir, having regard to what I will say later, I should point out that he then went on to say that:

It has been suggested that the principle of the *King* v.

Burgess may provide a method of amending the Constitution without the approval of the people. But this [he went on to say] is merely a rhetorical statement. . . .

(Well, sir, as one who has, in his time, occasionally lapsed or risen into rhetoric, I wince!)
And then he continued:

It has to be remembered that when, for instance, the Commonwealth enters into a convention as a member of the International Labour Organization and ratifies the obligations specified therein, such obligations are binding in international law, so that, when subsequently the Commonwealth passes legislation giving effect throughout the Commonwealth to the convention, it is not 'amending the Constitution', but acting strictly within it.

Well, sir, nobody can be dogmatic about the future course of decision on this great matter, though I am bound to say that I think the trend will most certainly be towards the strengthening of the central power. All I want to do is to point out how dramatic a change *in fact* would be made in the distribution of powers by the adoption of what I will call, with respect, 'the Evatt Doctrine'. Let us take his own example of labour conditions. For many years most of us in Australia have gone along under the impression that, apart from what we might do under its limited trade and commerce power 'trade and commerce with other countries, and among the States' and of course in its own territories, the only substantive Commonwealth industrial power was in Section 51, sub-section xxxv, 'conciliation and arbitration for the prevention and settlement of industrial disputes extending beyond the limits of any one State'.
Now that was a limited power, and those limits have been classified by a long line of judicial decisions. I can summarize them in a paragraph or two:

1. Parliament can set up conciliators and arbitrators to prevent or settle interstate disputes, but it cannot deal with disputes itself. It cannot make a law prescribing rates of pay or hours of work in an industry (except of course in its own territory). It cannot, except in a territory, or in relation to its own direct employees . . . deal with 'equal pay';

2. The dispute must be 'industrial', a word which has now been given a pretty wide interpretation, embracing a number of activities which would once have been regarded as 'professional';

3. The dispute must have an inter-State character.

The system of compulsory arbitration has, on the whole, worked well in Australia, largely because the judges and commissioners have been regarded by the general public as impartial. When my great predecessor, Prime Minister Bruce, attempted in 1929 substantially to repeal the Commonwealth Conciliation and Arbitration Act he was defeated in the House and was devastatingly defeated in the subsequent General Election. And I need hardly add that nobody has made a similar attempt since.

It is my own considered opinion that most thoughtful people in Australia would not want the great issues of pay and hours of work, with their tremendous economic implications, dealt with by a political auction at a Federal Election. But admittedly this is a political opinion.

Now, it seems clear that under what I call the *Evatt* doctrine all this could be changed without altering one line of the Constitution. If a Commonwealth government favoured a thirty-six hour week and became a party to an international convention, however few the other parties might be prescribing a thirty-six hour week, then the Commonwealth Parliament would have power to enact a thirty-six hour week, presumably, if the convention said so, for all areas of industry, and without reference to the industrial tribunals at all.

You note that I have just said 'however few the other parties might be'.

I face up to the problem in this way because there is a great weight of pure logic in the *Evatt* doctrine. Is there any foundation for an argument that a bilateral treaty does not attract the external affairs power, but a multi-lateral treaty does? I think the answer to this question is, as we used to say in my Parliament, 'in the negative'. For, clearly, a constitutional power conferred upon the Commonwealth cannot sensibly be interpreted by saying that it extends to treaties or agreements with A, B, and C, but not with A *or* B *or* C.

And so (as it seems to me) the *Evatt* doctrine brings within the domestic legislative competence of the Commonwealth Parliament (so long as that Parliament adheres strictly to the terms of the treaty or agreement) any matters which have been dealt with in an agreement with *one* other country. Here, indeed, is an interesting prospect. The ways of the world are mysterious, but it is always on the cards that Australia and some other country will have advanced Socialist or Radical governments at the same time. A single treaty would dispose of problems which, heretofore, have been regarded in Australia as matters for the conciliation and arbitration tribunals, acting under the Commonwealth's limited industrial powers.

Take, for an example, the long controversy about 'equal pay' for men and women. The industrial tribunals have usually established some differential. The problem has been left to them.

But under the *Evatt* interpretation of the power, an I.L.O. convention favouring equal pay, adopted by the Commonwealth of Australia, would enable the Commonwealth Parliament to legislate direct. And the same, as I understand it, would be true in the case of a bilateral treaty with any other country.

Well, sir, I hope you won't mind my saying that I am not unacquainted with the political mind, which, I assure you, is not without ingenuity.

Let the *Evatt* interpretation be adopted by the Full High Court (and he would be a very bold man who denied the possibility), and I have no doubt that many domestic problems so far regarded as not within Commonwealth power will be made the subject matter of some international agreement for the very purpose of attracting Commonwealth legislative power.

And so regarded and so employed, the power over 'external affairs' would be seen more and more as a power over 'internal affairs', and provide us with what our late friend W. S. Gilbert called a 'most ingenious paradox'.

True, political opponents could object that such procedures were being adopted for the sole, and, as they would say, improper purpose of extending the limits of Commonwealth power; but in retrospect, and I speak with utter ignorance of what your Supreme Court might do but with some idea of what the High Court of Australia might do, I really cannot see any court examining motives for government action, if on the face of it that action is found to come within some head of granted power.

Of course, it is quite true that the *Burgess* case can be readily enough distinguished. The regulation of civil aviation, in which great international operations occur, and international aircraft land in your country and mine, requires uniformity of flying rules if the public safety is to be protected.

In short, it is clearly a matter of definitely international character; the task of arguing that the ratification and application of an international convention dealing with it did not fall within the expression 'external affairs' was so difficult that all the judges rejected the argument.

It is not so clear, on the face of it, that an international document relating to, say, labour conditions inside each of the contracting countries would fall within the expression. For while the contemplation of a shorter working week in Ghana may give to some right-minded Australian or American observer a feeling of satisfaction, it is not easy to see that it has any bearing upon what goes on in Australia or in America, except in the most remote economic or philosophical sense.

Yet, as I have said, the logic of the *Evatt* reasoning possesses great force. Where do we draw the line? Can we fashion a series of criteria which will enable us to classify some arrangements as 'external affairs', and others, equally entered into by the Government as not 'external affairs'? In the light of what tests would the courts, confronted by two treaties or conventions, both competently acceded to by the Government of the nation, say that one could be legislated about under the external affairs power, while the other could not?

I have tried to work out some test, some standard of differentiation, in my own mind, but with no very clear or satisfactory result.

Plainly, treaties may be made which create mutual obligations in respect of our political relations with another country. They would obviously fall within 'external affairs'.

Again, as I have said, an international convention in relation to air safety measures, in an era of rapidly increasing international air transport, has domestic consequences; but those consequences directly affect the safety of international flying. So again we have a clear case.

But a treaty or convention which is concerned to secure the acceptance of domestic rules which are purely domestic, and which have no bearing upon the international movement of people or traffic, or international political or economic or financial relations, may well be in a different category. But, sir, I admit the exquisite difficulties of definition. Clearly, as

Sir Owen Dixon said, a series of particular cases will need to be judicially decided.

But I sum up by saying this. It may well come to pass that the 'external affairs' power in the Commonwealth of Australia will serve to illustrate my general thesis, that the growth of Commonwealth power in the Australian Federation has in a most striking way been much more the result of judicial interpretation than of formal amendments to the Constitution itself.

Note: Since this lecture was delivered, the case of *Airlines of N.S.W. Ltd.* v. *N.S.W.* (No. 2) has been recorded in 113 C.L.R. 54. In that case, *Menzies J.*, at p. 136 made a reference to the scope of the External Affairs power which may suggest some limit to that power. He said:

'Under the Constitution, Section 51 (xxix) 'External Affairs', the Commonwealth has power to make laws to carry out its international obligations under a convention with other nations concerning international affairs. When, as here, a party to litigation, and the Commonwealth supporting that party, rely upon Section 5 (xxix) to authorize the making of the Commonwealth law in question, it must appear to this Court that the law is for the carrying out of obligations of that description.'

This appears to suggest that a distinction may be drawn between an international convention concerning external affairs and a convention concerned with affairs falling outside that description.

9

The Banking Powers of the Commonwealth
(With some Final General Observations)

As you know, these lectures have been given on a theme, the theme being the growth of Commonwealth or central power in the Australian Federation; a very remarkable process that has gone on particularly in the last forty years. And tonight I come to the last of these matters, which is the Banking Power of the Commonwealth.

The Commonwealth Constitution in Section 51, confers powers on the Parliament of the Commonwealth to make laws for the peace, order, and good government of the Commonwealth with respect to,

First of all, trade and commerce with other countries, and among the States. That sounds rather comprehensive, but it turned out not to be.

Then,

(xii) Currency, coinage, and legal tender.
(xiii) Banking, other than State banking; also State banking extending beyond the limits of the State concerned, the incorporation of banks, and the issue of paper money.

The exercise of these powers may be affected by the Financial Agreement under Section 105A, about which I spoke earlier, and is subject to Section 92. Section 92 is one of those 'guarantee' constitutional provisions with which you are so familiar in your own country—'trade, commerce and intercourse between the states shall be absolutely free'.

K

And in Sub-section (xx), 'Foreign corporations, and trading or financial corporations formed within the limits of the Commonwealth'.

And in Sub-section (xxxix), 'Matters incidental to the execution of any power vested by this Constitution in the Parliament . . . or in the Government of the Commonwealth'.

Now, sir, the interesting thing about these powers is that while they are in some ways narrow, and in one way (the meaning of banking) somewhat vague, the Commonwealth has, under them and over a lengthy period, been able to build up a relatively far-reaching and in some ways adequate system of monetary and exchange control. This, you may at once say, demonstrates not the growth of power, but the exercise of power. This is true enough. But the real significance of the matter appears when we add this measure of control over monetary matters to those other great developments under Section 96 and Uniform Taxation and the Financial Agreement which I have endeavoured to explain in my earlier lectures. If we do this, we will see clearly the sources and nature of the Commonwealth's paramountcy in the fields of revenue, government capital provision, and (with some reservations) monetary and credit control.

A Government Bank named the Commonwealth Bank was established in 1911, during the Prime Ministership of Andrew Fisher. The Bank was placed under a Governor responsible only to Parliament. The Commonwealth Treasurer controlled the note issue.

There was some argument at the outset as to whether the Commonwealth Parliament could validly create a corporation, the Commonwealth Bank, without actual corporators. That matter was resolved in favour of validity.

My own view, after considering the records, is that its political promoters primarily intended it to compete for trading bank and savings bank business, and to do the Government's business at home and abroad, though some initial references were made to it becoming the 'Bank of banks'. The first Governor's policy—Denison Miller was the first Governor—envisaged that the Bank should become like the Bank of England; and he certainly did not enter into very active rivalry with the trading banks.

The principles of central banking were at that time not widely known.

But of necessity the first Great War, which broke out within a few years—in 1914—had a marked effect on the Bank's development. During the war it financially organized commodity pools for export products, it floated and managed War Loans for the Commonwealth Government, and became the Banker not only to the Commonwealth but to four State Governments. Clearly the movement towards Central Banking functions was on the way. Internationally, the early twenties saw much exchange of ideas about, and interest in central banking, and this had its impact in Australia.

In 1920 the note issue was removed from the control of the Treasurer, a control which he had exercised since 1910, and given to the Note Issue Department of the Bank. A gold reserve against the note issue was prescribed. And so central banking functions were arriving.

In 1924 a Commonwealth Bank Act was passed. Its express object was to encourage the Bank's development as a Central Bank. The then Treasurer put the matter compendiously in these words; I quote them:

A very great power is exercised by banks in the creation of credit, in their control over business, and in the effect of their policy on wages as well as upon other conditions. Changes in banking disturb the whole community and, under the divided control of banking which exists now, changes may be made which are not in the best interests of the community. The remedy is to be found in the co-ordination of banking effort by means of a central bank.

Well, the Act created a Board of Directors to control both the Bank and the note issue. It also required what I will call the private trading banks—this is an expression with which we are familiar in Australia—to settle exchanges through the Commonwealth Bank. This legislation did not produce all of its expected results. It was clearly designed to enhance the prestige of the Commonwealth Bank and to provide a framework for voluntary co-operation with other banks on the model of the operations of the Bank of England.

I have always thought personally that the British system works well, not on a foundation of compulsion, but on an established practice of mutual understanding and consultation. In Australia, we lean towards compulsion, and we have a dubious habit of thinking that you can persuade best if you wield a big stick.

In another respect, the analogy of the Bank of England was imperfect. It was thought that the placing of emphasis on the Commonwealth Bank's powers in respect of bills of exchange would mean that the Bank could and would use those powers, as the Bank of England does through its Bank Discount Rate, to influence or control credit. But the fact was that trade bills played a very small role in Australian business.

Well, as I am not writing a history of banking in Australia, I will summarize the later course of events by saying that, from 1929 on the inexorable demands of the Depression years controlled these events. Under legislation, the Commonwealth Bank secured control of gold in Australia whether held by private trading banks or State Banks or the public.

This measure was enacted under Section 51 (xii) of the Constitution, the 'currency' power, and was therefore not subject to the limitations on the banking power, which, as we have seen, specifically excluded State banking. An agreement was made with the trading banks for the mobilizaton of so much of their London reserves as was necessary to meet Government interest and certain other Government payments abroad.

Soon afterwards, the trading banks having failed to agree on a formula for determining the exchange rate, and being, in the nature of things, unable to control an 'outside market' which was becoming competitive and, from their point of view, damaging, the Commonwealth assumed control over the exchange rate and exercised exchange control.

In 1935, when I was Commonwealth Attorney-General, the Government appointed a Royal Commission to inquire into the banking and monetary systems of Australia. The Commission reported in 1937. It pointed out that the Federal Parliament must be ultimately responsible for monetary policy, and that in consequence any disagreement between the Government and the Commonwealth Bank about the policy to be followed by banks should be settled in the Government's favour. With some variations in procedure, this principle has since been established by legislation.

The Commission also recommended that the Commonwealth Bank should be given access to the overseas reserves of the trading banks and that those banks should be required to maintain minimum deposits with the Commonwealth Bank. The time was to come when both propositions, in substance, were adopted.

In the Second World War (that is to say, for us, 1939–45) a great development occurred. The defence powers, about which I spoke some time ago, operated in their immense plenitude. The powers given to the Commonwealth Bank included a virtual monopoly of exchange; the power to call up into 'special accounts' with itself increases in trading bank deposits, in order to control bank liquidity; power to direct trading bank advance policy; power to fix interest rates and to obtain information; power, in effect, to control bank profits by supervising trading bank investments, as part of a general wartime control of investments.

Well, just before the end of the war came the Banking Act, 1945, one aspect of which I discussed in an earlier lecture on the *Engineers' Case*. This Act incorporated the main aspects of the wartime regulations. It also provided that in the event of a dispute between the Treasurer and the Bank about monetary policies, the opinion of the Treasurer was to prevail. The Board was abolished, and an Advisory Council was substituted. The note issue gold reserve was abolished. The Bank was, under the Act, obliged to compete for trading bank business.

My own party, then in Opposition, but hopelessly outnumbered, promised that if we came back into office we would restore Board control and resolve differences by reference to Parliament, not to the Treasurer.

I have already mentioned the issue of Bank nationalization, and how it arose. The High Court's principal decision was that the Act violated Section 92 of the Constitution because it was contrary to the guarantee of absolute freedom of interstate trade, commerce, and intercourse. And the Privy Council, on appeal, declined to disturb this decision. I shall come back to that matter a little later.

When the Opposition, under my leadership, came into office in December 1949, we introduced a Commonwealth Bank Bill reconstituting a Bank Board, and repealing the Act of 1947, which was the nationalizing Act. We had trouble with an opposition-controlled Senate, secured a double dissolution of both Houses under the Constitution, and then passed our law.

Later, in 1953, after reviewing the legislation, we enacted several changes in the Commonwealth Bank structure, which were made complete by further legislation in 1957, the main features of which were:

1. A central Bank, to be called the Reserve Bank, was established, whose functions are related solely to central banking. Of the existing activities of the old Commonwealth

Bank, only the Rural Credits Department remains with the Reserve Bank.

2. There was a deep resistance by the trading banks to receiving orders from a central Bank which itself carried on, in strong competition with them, its own trading bank activities.

We were convinced that the effective working of the Reserve Bank on a basis of friendly co-operation required that the Commonwealth Bank's trading activities should be separated out, and placed under a separate Government Corporation which would be subject to exactly the same controls as those which applied to the private trading banks.

And we therefore, after some conflict with the Senate, which was resolved after the election of 1958, set up a new Commonwealth Banking Corporation, controlled by a separate Board, functioning independently of the Reserve Bank Board. Under this Corporation there are three Banks, the Commonwealth Trading Bank, the Commonwealth Savings Bank, and the Commonwealth Development Bank, the last-named being to provide finance for primary production and industrial development in circumstances where finance would not otherwise be available, through ordinary banking channels, on reasonable or suitable terms and conditions.

At the same time a Banking Act was passed. The previous Special Accounts system was replaced by a Statutory Reserve Deposit system. Under this system, the Reserve Bank can require the Trading Banks to lodge sums with it without limit, provided that forty-five days' notice must be given if the proportion of a trading bank's deposits to be lodged with the Reserve Bank exceeds 25 per cent. A uniform proportion of deposits is to apply to all major trading banks, including the Commonwealth Trading Bank. There were further provisions which enable savings banks to be conducted by the trading banks.

Well, so much for the history; it will be easier to read than to listen to. I now come back to a further consideration of the constitutional powers under which these things have been done.

The Commonwealth's powers over banking are, of course, limited by their own nature. Let me take the vexed case of what we usually called 'fringe' bankers. Now, we are all familiar with fringe banking, I know, but for most of us, it means that we are getting near the very edge of credit with the bank manager. In that sense, we are all familiar with it. But let me take the case of what we call, in Australia, 'fringe' bankers. A hire-purchase finance company receives deposits, usually on fairly short term or, quite possibly, at call, and at high rates of interest; higher than any normal bank could possibly pay without demanding very high overdraft rates from its customers. The finance company advances money to enable purchases of motor vehicles, domestic equipment, and the like, on hire purchase terms, at effective rates of interest which are very high—for the risks must be high—and, of course, agreeably embodied, for the benefit of housewives, in total lump sums.

Well, such a company does not provide cheque accounts or otherwise operate as a bank, except that it borrows money and lends it out.

Is this a 'bank'? Does it carry on 'banking'? Now this question has not been tested in the Courts. If and when it is, and the question is answered in the affirmative, the operations and control of the Reserve Bank will be extended.

But, as the matter now stands, the Commonwealth's powers over interest rates are restricted:

(a) It has powers in relation to interest rates on public loan issues, by virtue of its position in the Loan Council, to which I referred in an earlier lecture.

(b) It has powers over the rates of interest to be paid or

charged by the banks or in relation to banking operations. These are exercised in practice through the
Reserve Bank, which of course maintains regular
contact with the trading banks.

(*c*) Apart from the Government's Loan Council activities,
the Reserve Bank can conduct open market operations,
buying or selling public securities, which influence the
monetary supply but also serve to some extent as a
regulator of the effective yield on Government Bonds
on the Stock Exchanges and so have an effect on the
rates of interest which the Loan Council may decide
to offer on a new loan issue.

But one of the disabilities under which the reserve bank,
and through it the trading bank, suffers, is that, so long as
the 'fringe' institutions are outside these powers there
remains a large, and occasionally growing area of interest
rates which is outside the scope of general interest rate
policies, which certainly limits the efficacy of those policies
and may, to a perceptible degree, frustrate them or bring
undue pressure to bear on them.

In this way, the central banking activities of the Reserve
Bank are limited.

Another limitation upon the banking powers of the
Commonwealth Parliament was firmly established in what
is now known as *The Banking Case*, the High Court judgments
being reported in (1948) 76 C.L.R. 1, and that of the Judicial
Committee of the Privy Council in (1949) 79 C.L.R. 497.
I mentioned this famous matter very briefly in my lecture on
the *Engineers' Case*. I will now deal with it more elaborately.

The Chifley Labour Government was stung by the High
Court decision in the *Melbourne Corporation Case* (1947),
74 C.L.R. 31, invalidating the provisions of the Banking
Act 1945, which, as you will recall if you are hardy enough
to remember my earlier lectures, provided that without the

consent of the Commonwealth Treasurer a bank should not conduct banking business for a State, or for any authority of a State, including a local governing authority.

It decided to 'go the whole hog', and nationalize the Banks. It set out to do this by the Banking Act 1947. Briefly stated, the objects of this measure were, as stated in Section 3, the expansion of the banking business of the Commonwealth Bank as a publicly-owned Bank; the taking over by the Commonwealth Bank of the banking business in Australia of private banks, and the acquisition of property used in that business; and the prohibition of the carrying on of banking business in Australia by private banks.

This Act was challenged by the private banks on a variety of grounds, one of which is of outstanding importance for my general thesis. That was that the Act violated Section 92 of the Constitution, guaranteeing the absolute freedom of inter-State trade, commerce and intercourse.

Now, the facts were, as stated by *Dixon J.* (at pp. 379–80):

> the existing system of private banking maintains an Australia-wide business upon which its whole structure rests. It sustains with respect to the transfer of money or bank credit the greater part of the commerce of the country. Branches and agencies of the various private banks are distributed over the Commonwealth. . . . The volume of the banking transactions which cross State lines is, of course, widely different with different banks. . . . But the total quantity for all banks is very large.

This means that:

> the business of the trading banks necessarily includes the constant inter-State transmission of funds and transfer of credit; constant business communication and intercourse among the States.

[144]

It was argued for the Commonwealth that the 'trade, commerce, and intercourse' protected by Section 92 extended to the transfer from one State to another of nothing but commodities and persons. This contention was rejected as unwarranted by a full interpretation of the words. It was, indeed, described by *Dixon J.* as a 'reactionary interpretation'.

The Judicial Committee expressly agreed, saying:

> The business of banking, consisting of the creation and transfer of loans, the purchase and disposal of investments and other kindred activities, is a part of the trade, commerce and intercourse of a modern society, and, in so far as it is carried on by means of inter-State transactions, is within the ambit of Section 92. Upon this part of the case they respectfully adopt the language and reasoning of *Dixon J.*, to which they can add nothing. (79 C.L.R., at 632-3.)

In the result, and I omit reference to many refinements which were dealt with in the arguments and judgments, it was clearly established that Section 92 invalidated the Banking Act so far as it purported to empower the total prohibition of private banking, both intra-State and inter-State. You will at once appreciate that, as a political sort of animal, I am not complaining about that decision. I attacked the policy of bank nationalization from one end of the country to the other, and made long, and I thought powerful, speeches in Parliament, where I could occasionally think I had won the debate in terms of argument, but lost it when the numbers went up.

So it was joy to me when the Courts spoke.

The limitation imposed by Section 92 saved the trading banks from destruction and thus preserved competitive trading banking in Australia. But subject to such express Constitutional provisions (and all of the Commonwealth's powers are limited in the same way) the Banking powers have the degree of amplitude which I have described. Their exercise has had far-reaching and important effects. It has strengthened the position of the Commonwealth in the fields of monetary and credit management.

I could summarize this aspect of the matter in three propositions:

1. The management of monetary conditions through the operation of the Reserve Bank has necessarily a large influence upon the availability of money for public works, and upon taxation.

2. Measures of monetary and credit control have been and are important instruments for giving effect to national economic policy.

3. The fact that the Commonwealth Government, by such means as the discounting of Treasury Bills, has access to the Reserve Bank for credit to meet budgetary needs, puts the Commonwealth into a very different position from that of the States, whose access to such facilities is limited and in fact subject to Commonwealth control.

In these lectures I have done my best, within the limits imposed by time and my own capacity, to bring into some reasonable perpective the growth of Commonwealth powers in the Australian Federation. It has been, indeed, a remarkable growth.

But, as students in a Federal system yourselves, you will not need to be told by me that the powers of the central Parliament and Government are in no sense absolute. We frequently find that, in an effort to devise and give effect to a national economic and financial policy, we encounter deficiencies of power which can be very irritating but must be accepted as in the very nature of federalism.

I will illustrate this by a comparatively recent example.

Considerable as the banking powers have turned out to be, and wide as the Commonwealth's authority has become over both the revenue and the capital resources of the States, it has proved necessary to point out publicly that the Commonwealth's financial and economic powers are not unlimited. There are still some popular superstitions to the contrary, superstitions which have on occasion dimmed the vision even of the industrial tribunals.

Thus, in his judgment on the Basic Wage application of 1950, in the course of which he gave the deciding vote which added twenty shillings a week to the Basic Wage—a very large increase—the late Mr Justice Foster, at p. 797 of 68 *Commonwealth Arbitration Reports*, said:

> I shall be concerned with the fact that an increase in the basic wage which will inevitably permeate the whole wage structure will increase prices and so add its modicum of inflationary pressure, but inflation and its control are matters for the Government. . . . I must assume that the proper authorities will take such steps as they are advised to safeguard the community from the effects of an inflation. . . .

This was an over-statement, or perhaps an over-assumption of the powers of the Commonwealth Government and Parliament. Mr Justice Foster's view was challenged by counsel for the Commonwealth in the *Basic Wage Case* of 1956.

He pointed out that no government in any country has found it easy to deal with inflationary conditions; in a Federation the problem was even more complex, because of the division of powers.

He indicated that, while the pressure of investment upon resources could produce inflation, and while the concentration of that pressure upon particular industries could produce economic distortions of a serious kind, the Commonwealth Parliament, except in time of war and for some limited time thereafter under the defence powers, has no power to regulate or control investment.

[147]

He dwelt on the limited nature of the Commonwealth's powers over interest rates, which I have discussed earlier, saying 'The limited character of the Commonwealth's power in relation to interest is sharply illustrated by the fact that the Commonwealth is unable to curb the mounting volume of hire-purchase'.

He conceded, properly, that taxation can be a powerful weapon. My own Government had used it very vigorously and with great temporary unpopularity in an attack on the inflation which grew in the very early fifties—to which I have referred. But he argued that the taking of fiscal measures to counteract an excess of purchasing power is not susceptible to precise use for precise purposes. This is of course quite true. In an earlier lecture I quoted the Australian Constitutional provisions which prevent discrimination between States or parts of States (Section 51 (ii)), and the now well-established provision for uniform taxation. Economic conditions in individual States may vary, but as between one State and another taxation policy cannot. Again, of course, just as we are assured that the rain strikes the just and the unjust alike, so does the drought or fire or flood. In the result, counter inflationary increased taxes, direct or indirect, can inflict much individual hardship on people who, in their personal circumstances, are actually suffering an acute depression.

Counsel, to continue his argument, discussed the theoretically accurate proposition that by concerted action between all of them the Commonwealth and the six States could, subject of course to Section 92, exercise all the powers which the Government of a unitary State could wield. He properly dismissed this as both unreal and absurd. Governments and Parliaments are not accustomed to such unanimity, as you will have no difficulty in understanding. He concluded by saying:

The conception that the Government has ample power to deal with any inflation which some other authority might create or feed is completely inaccurate and, indeed, dangerous.

As to which I would say, in the well-known Australian idiom, 'too right'.

I now add some further observations of my own about the powers of the Commonwealth. It has no power over the rates of pay, or working hours, each of which can, of course, produce inflationary effects if they increase purchasing power and reduce the volume of production. Broadly, the Commonwealth can set up the arbitration tribunals, or destroy them. But, because of the nature of the power, it cannot order them what to do or alter what they have done.

Again, the volume and character of imported goods can affect the supply-demand position in Australia very materially. But this question is closely associated with customs tariff policy. Though this is a matter within the full and indeed exclusive control of the Commonwealth, the Government's hands have been tied partly by trade treaties and partly by a long-accepted national policy, accepted, I think, on both sides of Parliament, under which the Commonwealth sets up a Tariff Board, which investigates and reports on all applications for duties. In practice, governments accept the recommendations of the Board except in rare cases and under special circumstances.

The use of interest rates control as a means of inflation control (or deflation control) is, of course, well recognized. But in this matter, as I have pointed out earlier, the Commonwealth powers are not comprehensive, flexible, or selective.

There are forces of nature which no Constitution can control, and which affect both inflation and deflation. In many parts of Australia, climatic conditions are uncertain.

We recently had a great drought in areas which normally produce large numbers of sheep and cattle. The effects of this drought will be felt for years. Other areas are subject to periodic flooding; while we have had from time to time bitter experience of devastating bush-fires. Such events produce great individual losses and heavy government domestic expenditures; but they also adversely affect our export income. If they happen to coincide with falls in the prices the world markets will pay for our staple products, our overseas funds run down. This movement is reflected in the liquidity of the Australian banking structure and the availability of industrial and commercial credit. On the other hand, overseas events, such as the Korean War in 1950, can set up abnormal demands and steeply rising prices, as happened when very great increases in the price of wool—our greatest single item—came about as a result of a buying boom, largely generated in the United States. A very great inflation occurred, which evoked the most severe Commonwealth Budget in my experience. We increased taxes, we budgeted for a large surplus, and we 'froze' a proportion of the wool-growers' incomes. As you have wool-growers, nothing like as efficient as ours, and protect their interests by an astonishing import duty on wool—which hits Australia—you will, even in the groves of the Virginian Academy, understand that this was not popular. That was, to an extent, because many wool-growers, with suddenly massive gross incomes, forgot about taxes and bought expensive motor-cars, and sent their families on tours to Europe. They came back to us, politically, when they found that the 'spreading' of their incomes worked out, over a few years, in favour of their own stability.

The real point is that, if a Government in Australia wishes either to counteract inflation or promote expansion to defeat depression (or 'recession', a much more agreeable word), it will suffer from either a deficiency of power or the need to resort to severe measures, not very selective in their nature, and always unpopular.

But this cannot possibly concern you. With your traditional courtesy, you have permitted an old politician to be a little reminiscent.

Before I conclude, I have an apology or an explanation to make; I do not know which. I have made no elaborate reference to the famous Section 92 of the Australian Constitution, which provides that:

> On the imposition of uniform duties of customs, trade, commerce, and intercourse among the States, whether by means of internal carriage or ocean navigation, shall be absolutely free.

This has been one of the most litigated sections in the Constitution. At one stage in its judicial history (which, I may say, illustrates the dangers and ambiguities of general provisions couched in popular language!) it was thought that Section 92 did not bind the Commonwealth, and was specifically directed to the States.

This view was finally rejected in *James* v. *The Commonwealth* (1936), A.C. 578, a case in which I appeared with a considerable lack of success. But for this decision, I would have felt compelled to examine the series of cases in which this Section has been judicially interpreted, since such an examination would have been appropriate to a study of the growth of *Commonwealth power*. For more laws have been invalidated by the application of Section 92 than (as I am impudent enough to believe) the draftsmen of the Constitution ever dreamed of. And if they had been State laws only, the expansionary effect on Commonwealth powers, particularly the trade and commerce powers, would have been considerable. But, since Section 92 is now seen to bear equally upon Commonwealth and States, I have not thought

L

it appropriate or necessary to write an excursus on the Section for purposes of the general theme of these lectures. For this relief, you and I may give 'much thanks'.

I am grateful to you for the courtesy with which you have listened to these lectures. I am conscious of their imperfections. It was, indeed, impossible to cover so wide a field in a few necessarily brief essays.

I have, in fact, tried to perform a pilot exercise, which will, I hope, serve to stimulate more elaborate studies by lawyers and political scientists in future. My central purpose has been to demonstrate a great truth about the study of a federal Constitution. That truth is that although it is a sound rule to go back to the language of the Constitution—*melius est petere fontes quam sectare rivulos*—it is a mistake to think that a Constitution is something rigid and inflexible, to be interpreted like any ordinary Statute, to have a meaning fixed for all time. I have defended legalism as something inherent in federalism. But it is not inconsistent with the legalistic approach to recognize that a written Constitution is an expressed scheme of government designed to give a basic structure in a changing world; not designed to inhibit growth in a growing world, nor to make the contemporary world subject to the political, social, or economic ideas of a bygone age.

In the case of Australia, the great corrective has been, not to ignore or reject the language of the Constitution—for this would be unauthorized and destructive of principle—but to adopt liberal interpretations of that language, preserving the basic constitutional principles that a Constitution, though written and adopted at a much earlier time, was intended to be a living instrument for generations and centuries to come.

What I have said to you about the remarkable, and, I think, un-anticipated growth of central power in Australia, illustrates the truth of these views.

Speaking in a University founded by that great and versatile and far-sighted genius, Thomas Jefferson, speaking in the very shadow of his name and memory, I can only hope that some of the things I have said would have merited his approval as a serious contribution to politico-legal knowledge.

APPENDIX

The Commonwealth of Australia Constitution Act

(63 & 64 VICTORIA, CHAPTER 12)
An Act to constitute the Commonwealth of Australia.
[9th July, 1900.]

WHEREAS the people of New South Wales, Victoria, South Australia, Queensland, and Tasmania, humbly relying on the blessing of Almighty God, have agreed to unite in one indissoluble Federal Commonwealth under the Crown of the United Kingdom of Great Britain and Ireland, and under the Constitution hereby established:

And whereas it is expedient to provide for the admission into the Commonwealth of other Australasian Colonies and possessions of the Queen:

Be it therefore enacted by the Queen's Most Excellent Majesty, by and with the advice and consent of the Lords Spiritual and Temporal, and Commons, in this present Parliament assembled, and by the authority of the same, as follows:

Short title

1. This Act may be cited as the Commonwealth of Australia Constitution Act.

Act to extend to the Queen's successors

2. The provisions of this Act referring to the Queen shall extend to Her Majesty's heirs and successors in the sovereignty of the United Kingdom.

NOTE.—This print of the Constitution Act contains all the alterations of the Constitution which have been made up to 1st January, 1961. The Acts by which the Constitution was altered are the Constitution Alteration (Senate Elections) 1906 (assented to 3rd April, 1907); the Constitution Alteration (State Debts) 1909 (assented to 6th August, 1910); the Constitution Alteration (State Debts) 1928 (assented to 13th February, 1929); and the Constitution Alteration (Social Services) 1946 (assented to 19th December, 1946).

3. It shall be lawful for the Queen, with the advice of the Privy Council, to declare by proclamation* that, on and after a day therein appointed, not being later than one year after the passing of this Act, the people of New South Wales, Victoria, South Australia, Queensland, and Tasmania, and also, if Her Majesty is satisfied that the people of Western Australia have agreed thereto, of Western Australia, shall be united in a Federal Commonwealth under the name of the Commonwealth of Australia. But the Queen may, at any time after the proclamation, appoint a Governor-General for the Commonwealth.

Proclamation of Commonwealth

4. The Commonwealth shall be established, and the Constitution of the Commonwealth shall take effect, on and after the day so appointed. But the Parliaments of the several colonies may at any time after the passing of this Act make any such laws, to come into operation on the day so appointed, as they might have made if the Constitution had taken effect at the passing of this Act.

Commencement of Act

5. This Act, and all laws made by the Parliament of the Commonwealth under the Constitution, shall be binding on the courts, judges, and people of every State and of every part of the Commonwealth, notwithstanding anything in the laws of any State; and the laws of the Commonwealth shall be in force on all British ships, the Queen's ships of war excepted, whose first port of clearance and whose port of destination are in the Commonwealth.†

Operation of the Constitution and laws

6. 'The Commonwealth' shall mean the Commonwealth of Australia as established under this Act.

Definitions

'The States' shall mean such of the colonies of New South Wales, New Zealand, Queensland, Tasmania, Victoria, Western Australia, and South Australia, including the northern territory of South Australia, as

* The proclamation declared that on and after the first day of January, One thousand nine hundred and one, the people of New South Wales, Victoria, South Australia, Queensland, Tasmania and Western Australia should be united in a Federal Commonwealth under the name of the Commonwealth of Australia; *see Gazette*, 1901, p. 1 and Commonwealth Statutory Rules 1901–1956, Vol. V, p. 5300.

† *Cf.* section 3 of the Statute of Westminster, 1931 (p. 36 *infra*).

for the time being are parts of the Commonwealth, and such colonies or territories as may be admitted into or established by the Commonwealth as States; and each of such parts of the Commonwealth shall be called 'a State'.

'Original States' shall mean such States as are parts of the Commonwealth at its establishment.

Repeal of Federal Council Act

48 & 49 Vict. c. 60

7. The Federal Council of Australasia Act, 1885, is hereby repealed, but so as not to affect any laws passed by the Federal Council of Australasia and in force at the establishment of the Commonwealth.

Any such law may be repealed* as to any State by the Parliament of the Commonwealth, or as to any colony not being a State by the Parliament thereof.

Application of Colonial Boundaries Act

58 & 59 Vict. c. 34

8. After the passing of this Act the Colonial Boundaries Act, 1895, shall not apply to any colony which becomes a State of the Commonwealth; but the Commonwealth shall be taken to be a self-governing colony for the purposes of that Act.

Constitution

9. The Constitution of the Commonwealth shall be as follows:

THE CONSTITUTION

This Constitution is divided as follows:

Chapter   I   The Parliament
     Part   I   General
     Part   II   The Senate
     Part   III   The House of Representatives
     Part   IV   Both Houses of the Parliament
     Part   V   Powers of the Parliament
Chapter   II   The Executive Government
Chapter   III   The Judicature
Chapter   IV   Finance and Trade
Chapter   V   The States
Chapter   VI   New States
Chapter   VII   Miscellaneous
Chapter VIII   Alteration of the Constitution
The Schedule.

* The following Commonwealth Acts have repealed Acts passed by the Federal Council of Australasia:

     Pearl Fisheries Act 1952–1953, section 3.
     Service and Execution of Process Act 1901–1958, section 2.

CHAPTER I

THE PARLIAMENT

PART I GENERAL

1. The legislative power of the Commonwealth shall be vested in a Federal Parliament, which shall consist of the Queen, a Senate, and a House of Representatives, and which is hereinafter called 'The Parliament', or 'The Parliament of the Commonwealth'.

2. A Governor-General appointed by the Queen shall be Her Majesty's representative in the Commonwealth, and shall have and may exercise in the Commonwealth during the Queen's pleasure, but subject to this Constitution, such powers and functions of the Queen as Her Majesty may be pleased to assign to him.

3. There shall be payable to the Queen out of the Consolidated Revenue fund of the Commonwealth, for the salary of the Governor-General, an annual sum which, until the Parliament otherwise provides, shall be ten thousand pounds.

The salary of a Governor-General shall not be altered during his continuance in office.

4. The provisions of this Constitution relating to the Governor-General extend and apply to the Governor-General for the time being, or such person as the Queen may appoint to administer the Government of the Commonwealth; but no such person shall be entitled to receive any salary from the Commonwealth in respect of any other office during his administration of the Government of the Commonwealth.

5. The Governor-General may appoint such times for holding the sessions of the Parliament as he thinks fit, and may also from time to time, by Proclamation or otherwise, prorogue the Parliament, and may in like manner dissolve the House of Representatives.

After any general election the Parliament shall be summoned to meet not later than thirty days after the day appointed for the return of the writs.

The Parliament shall be summoned to meet not later than six months after the establishment of the Commonwealth.

6. There shall be a session of the Parliament once at least in every year, so that twelve months shall not intervene between the last sitting of the Parliament in one session and its first sitting in the next session.

PART II THE SENATE

7. The Senate shall be composed of senators for each State, directly chosen by the people of the State, voting, until the Parliament otherwise provides, as one electorate.

But until the Parliament of the Commonwealth otherwise provides, the Parliament of the State of Queensland, if that State be an Original State, may make laws dividing the State into divisions and determining the number of senators to be chosen for each division, and in the absence of such provision the State shall be one electorate.

Until the Parliament otherwise provides there shall be six senators for each Original State. The Parliament may make laws increasing or diminishing the number of senators for each State,* but so that equal representation of the several Original States shall be maintained and that no Original State shall have less than six senators.

The senators shall be chosen for a term of six years, and the names of the senators chosen for each State shall be certified by the Governor to the Governor-General.

8. The qualification of electors of senators shall be in each State that which is prescribed by this Constitution, or by the Parliament, as the qualification for electors of members of the House of Representatives; but in the choosing of senators each elector shall vote only once.

9. The Parliament of the Commonwealth may make laws prescribing the method of choosing senators, but so that the method shall be uniform for all the States. Subject to any such law, the Parliament of each State may

---

* The number of senators for each State was increased to ten by the Representation Act 1948, section 4.

make laws* prescribing the method of choosing the
senators for that State.

The Parliament of a State may make laws for determin-   Times and
ing the times and places of elections of senators for the   places
State.

10. Until the Parliament otherwise provides, but   Application of
subject to this Constitution, the laws in force in each   State laws
State, for the time being, relating to elections for the more
numerous House of the Parliament of the State shall, as
nearly as practicable, apply to elections of senators for
the State.

11. The Senate may proceed to the despatch of   Failure to
business, notwithstanding the failure of any State to   choose senators
provide for its representation in the Senate.

12. The Governor of any State may cause writs to be   Issue of writs
issued for elections of senators for the State. In case of
the dissolution of the Senate the writs shall be issued

* The following State Acts have been passed in pursuance of the powers conferred by section 9 :—

State	Number	Short Title	How Affected
New South Wales	No. 73, 1900	Federal Elections Act, 1900	Sections 2, 3, 4, 5 and 6 and the Schedule repealed by No. 9, 1903; wholly repealed by No. 41, 1912
New South Wales	No. 9, 1903	Senators' Elections Act, 1903	Amended by No. 75, 1912
New South Wales	No. 75, 1912	Senators' Elections (Amendment) Act, 1912	—
Victoria	No. 1715	Federal Elections Act, 1900	Repealed by No. 1860
Victoria	No. 1860	Senate Elections (Times and Places) Act, 1903	Repealed and re-enacted by No. 2723
Victoria	No. 2723	Senate Elections (Times and Places) Act, 1915	Repealed and re-enacted by No. 3769
Victoria	No. 3769	Senate Elections (Times and Places) Act, 1928	Repealed and re-enacted by No. 6365
Victoria	No. 6365	Senate Elections Act, 1958	
Queensland	64 Vic. No. 25	The Parliament of the Commonwealth Elections Act and the Elections Acts, 1885 to 1898, Amendment Act of 1900	Operation exhausted
Queensland	3 Edw. VII. No. 6	The Elections of Senators Act of 1903	—
South Australia	No. 834	The Election of Senators Act, 1903	—
Western Australia	No. 11, 1903	Election of Senators Act, 1903	Amended by No. 27, 1912
Western Australia	No. 27, 1912	Election of Senators Amendment Act, 1912	—
Tasmania	64 Vic. No. 59	The Federal Elections Act, 1900	Repealed by 26 Geo. V. No. 3
Tasmania	3 Edw. VII. No. 5	The Election of Senators Act, 1903	Repealed by 26 Geo. V. No. 3
Tasmania	26 Geo. V. No. 3	Senate Elections Act, 1935	—

within ten days from the proclamation of such dissolution.

Rotation of senators
Altered by No. 1, 1907, s. 2

13. As soon as may be after the Senate first meets, and after each first meeting of the Senate following a dissolution thereof, the Senate shall divide the senators chosen for each State into two classes, as nearly equal in number as practicable; and the places of the senators of the first class shall become vacant at the expiration of three years, and the places of those of the second class at the expiration of six years, from the beginning of their term of service; and afterwards the places of senators shall become vacant at the expiration of six years from the beginning of their term of service.

The election to fill vacant places shall be made within one year before the places are to become vacant.

For the purposes of this section the term of service of a senator shall be taken to begin on the first day of July following the day of his election, except in the cases of the first election and of the election next after any dissolution of the Senate, when it shall be taken to begin on the first day of July preceding the day of his election.

Further provision for rotation

14. Whenever the number of senators for a State is increased or diminished, the Parliament of the Commonwealth may make such provision for the vacating of the places of senators for the State as it deems necessary to maintain regularity in the rotation.*

Casual vacancies

15. If the place of a senator becomes vacant before the expiration of his term of service, the Houses of Parliament of the State for which he was chosen shall, sitting and voting together choose a person to hold the place until the expiration of the term, or until the election of a successor as hereinafter provided, whichever first happens. But if the Houses of Parliament of the State are not in session at the time when the vacancy is notified, the Governor of the State, with the advice of the Executive Council thereof, may appoint a person to hold the place until the expiration of fourteen days after the beginning of the next session of the Parliament of the State, or until the election of a successor, whichever first happens.

At the next general election of members of the House of

* *See* Representation Act 1948–1949, sections 4 and 5.

Representatives, or at the next election of senators for the State, whichever first happens, a successor shall, if the term has not then expired, be chosen to hold the place from the date of his election until the expiration of the term.

The name of any senator so chosen or appointed shall be certified by the Governor of the State to the Governor-General.

16. The qualifications of a senator shall be the same as those of a member of the House of Representatives. *Qualifications of senator*

17. The Senate shall, before proceeding to the despatch of any other business, choose a senator to be the President of the Senate; and as often as the office of President becomes vacant the Senate shall again choose a senator to be the President. *Election of President*

The President shall cease to hold his office if he ceases to be a senator. He may be removed from office by a vote of the Senate, or he may resign his office or his seat by writing addressed to the Governor-General

18. Before or during any absence of the President, the Senate may choose a senator to perform his duties in his absence. *Absence of President*

19. A senator may, by writing addressed to the President, or to the Governor-General if there is no President or if the President is absent from the Commonwealth, resign his place, which thereupon shall become vacant. *Resignation of senator*

20. The place of a senator shall become vacant if for two consecutive months of any session of the Parliament he, without the permission of the Senate, fails to attend the Senate. *Vacancy by absence*

21. Whenever a vacancy happens in the Senate, the President, or if there is no President or if the President is absent from the Commonwealth the Governor-General, shall notify the same to the Governor of the State in the representation of which the vacancy has happened. *Vacancy to be notified*

22. Until the Parliament otherwise provides, the presence of at least one-third of the whole number of the senators shall be necessary to constitute a meeting of the Senate for the exercise of its powers. *Quorum*

23. Questions arising in the Senate shall be determined by a majority of votes, and each senator shall have one vote. The President shall in all cases be entitled to a vote; and when the votes are equal the question shall pass in the negative.

PART III
HOUSE OF
REPRESENTA-
TIVES

Constitution of
House of
Representatives

PART III   THE HOUSE OF REPRESENTATIVES

24. The House of Representatives shall be composed of members directly chosen by the people of the Commonwealth, and the number of such members shall be, as nearly as practicable, twice the number of the senators.

The number of members chosen in the several States shall be in proportion to the respective numbers of their people, and shall, until the Parliament otherwise provides, be determined whenever necessary, in the following manner:

(i) A quota shall be ascertained by dividing the number of the people of the Commonwealth, as shown by the latest statistics of the Commonwealth, by twice the number of the senators:

(ii) The number of members to be chosen in each State shall be determined by dividing the number of the people of the State, as shown by the latest statistics of the Commonwealth, by the quota; and if on such division there is a remainder greater than one-half of the quota, one more member shall be chosen in the State.

But notwithstanding anything in this section, five members at least shall be chosen in each Original State.

25. For the purposes of the last section, if by the law of any State all persons of any race are disqualified from voting at elections for the more numerous House of the Parliament of the State, then, in reckoning the number of the people of the State or of the Commonwealth, persons of that race resident in that State shall not be counted.

26. Notwithstanding anything in section twenty-four, the number of members to be chosen in each State at the first election shall be as follows:

New South Wales   twenty-three

Victoria	twenty
Queensland	eight
South Australia	six
Tasmania	five

Provided that if Western Australia is an Original State, the numbers shall be as follows:

New South Wales	twenty-six
Victoria	twenty-three
Queensland	nine
South Australia	seven
Western Australia	five
Tasmania	five

27. Subject to this Constitution, the Parliament may make laws for increasing or diminishing the number of the members of the House of Representatives. <small>Alteration of number of members</small>

28. Every House of Representatives shall continue for three years from the first meeting of the House, and no longer, but may be sooner dissolved by the Governor-General. <small>Duration of House of Representatives</small>

29. Until the Parliament of the Commonwealth otherwise provides, the Parliament of any State may make laws* for determining the divisions in each State for which members of the House of Representatives may be chosen, and the number of members to be chosen for each division. A division shall not be formed out of parts of different States. <small>Electoral divisions</small>

In the absence of other provision, each State shall be one electorate.

---

* The following State Acts were passed in pursuance of the powers conferred by section 29, but ceased to be in force upon the enactment of the Commonwealth Electoral Act 1902:

State	Number	Short Title
New South Wales	No. 73, 1900	Federal Elections Act, 1900
Victoria	No. 1667	Federal House of Representatives Victorian Electorates Act, 1900
Queensland	64 Vic. No. 25	The Parliament of the Commonwealth Elections Act and The Elections Acts 1885 to 1898 Amendment Act of 1900
Western Australia	64 Vic. No. 6	Federal House of Representatives Western Australian Electorates Act, 1900

Qualification of electors

30. Until the Parliament otherwise provides, the qualification of electors of members of the House of Representatives shall be in each state that which is prescribed by the law of the State as the qualification of electors of the more numerous House of Parliament of the State; but in the choosing of members each elector shall vote only once.

Application of State laws

31. Until the Parliament otherwise provides, but subject to this Constitution, the laws in force in each State for the time being relating to elections for the more numerous House of the Parliament of the State shall, as nearly as practicable, apply to elections in the State of members of the House of Representatives.

Writs for general election

32. The Governor-General in Council may cause writs to be issued for general elections of members of the House of Representatives.

After the first general election, the writs shall be issued within ten days from the expiry of a House of Representatives or from the proclamation of a dissolution thereof.

Writs for vacancies

33. Whenever a vacancy happens in the House of Representatives, the Speaker shall issue his writ for the election of a new member, or if there is no Speaker or if he is absent from the Commonwealth the Governor-General in Council may issue the writ.

Qualifications of members

34. Until the Parliament otherwise provides, the qualifications of a member of the House of Representatives shall be as follows:—

(i) He must be of the full age of twenty-one years, and must be an elector entitled to vote at the election of members of the House of Representatives, or a person qualified to become such elector, and must have been for three years at the least a resident within the limits of the Commonwealth as existing at the time when he is chosen:

(ii) He must be a subject of the Queen, either natural-born or for at least five years naturalized under a law of the United Kingdom, or of a Colony which has become or becomes a State, or of the Commonwealth, or of a State.

[164]

35. The House of Representatives shall, before pro-Election of
Speaker
ceeding to the despatch of any other business, choose a
member to be the Speaker of the House, and as often as
the office of Speaker becomes vacant the House shall
again choose a member to be the Speaker.

The Speaker shall cease to hold his office if he ceases
to be a member. He may be removed from office by a
vote of the House, or he may resign his office or his seat
by writing addressed to the Governor-General.

36. Before or during any absence of the Speaker, Absence of
Speaker
the House of Representatives may choose a member to
perform his duties in his absence.

37. A member may by writing addressed to the Resignation of
member
Speaker, or to the Governor-General if there is no
Speaker or if the Speaker is absent from the Commonwealth, resign his place, which thereupon shall become
vacant.

38. The place of a member shall become vacant if Vacancy by
absence
for two consecutive months of any session of the Parliament he, without the permission of the House, fails to
attend the House.

39. Until the Parliament otherwise provides, the Quorum
presence of at least one-third of the whole number of
the members of the House of Representatives shall be
necessary to constitute a meeting of the House for the
exercise of its powers.

40. Questions arising in the House of Representatives Voting
in House of
Representatives
shall be determined by a majority of votes other than
that of the Speaker. The Speaker shall not vote unless
the numbers are equal, and then he shall have a casting
vote.

PART IV BOTH HOUSES OF THE PARLIAMENT
PART IV
BOTH HOUSES
OF THE
PARLIAMENT

41. No adult person who has or acquires a right to Right of
electors of
States
vote at elections for the more numerous House of the
Parliament of a State shall, while the right continues, be
prevented by any law of the Commonwealth from voting
at elections for either House of the Parliament of the
Commonwealth.

Oath or affirmation of allegiance

42. Every senator and every member of the House of Representatives shall before taking his seat make and subscribe before the Governor-General, or some person authorized by him, an oath or affirmation of allegiance in the form set forth in the schedule to this Constitution.

Member of one House ineligible for other

43. A member of either House of the Parliament shall be incapable of being chosen or of sitting as a member of the other House.

Disqualification

44. Any person who

(i) under any acknowledgment of allegiance, obedience, or adherence to a foreign power, or is a subject or a citizen or entitled to the rights or privileges of a subject or a citizen of a foreign power: or

(ii) Is attainted of treason, or has been convicted and is under sentence, or subject to be sentenced, for any offence punishable under the law of the Commonwealth or of a State by imprisonment for one year or longer: or

(iii) Is an undischarged bankrupt or insolvent: or

(iv) Holds any office of profit under the Crown, or any pension payable during the pleasure of the Crown out of any of the revenues of the Commonwealth: or

(v) Has any direct or indirect pecuniary interest in any agreement with the Public Service of the Commonwealth otherwise than as a member and in common with the other members of an incorporated company consisting of more than twenty-five persons:

shall be incapable of being chosen or of sitting as a senator or a member of the House of Representatives.

But sub-section (iv) does not apply to the office of any of the Queen's Ministers of State for the Commonwealth, or of any of the Queen's Ministers for a State, or to the receipt of pay, half-pay, or a pension by any person as an officer or member of the Queen's navy or army, or to the receipt of pay as an officer or member of the naval or military forces of the Commonwealth by any person whose services are not wholly employed by the Commonwealth.

45. If a senator or member of the House of Repre- Vacancy on
happening of
disqualification
sentatives—

(i) Becomes subject to any of the disabilities mentioned in the last preceding section: or

(ii) Takes the benefit, whether by assignment, com-
position, or otherwise, of any law relating to
bankrupt or insolvent debtors: or

(iii) Directly or indirectly takes or agrees to take any
fee or honorarium for services rendered to the
Commonwealth, or for services rendered in the
Parliament to any person or State:

his place shall thereupon become vacant.

46. Until the Parliament otherwise provides, any Penalty for
sitting when
disqualified
person declared by this Constitution to be incapable of
sitting as a senator or as a member of the House of
Representatives shall, for every day on which he so sits,
be liable to pay the sum of one hundred pounds to any
person who sues for it in any court of competent jurisdiction.

47. Until the Parliament otherwise provides, any Disputed
elections
question respecting the qualification of a senator or of a
member of the House of Representatives, or respecting
a vacancy in either House of the Parliament, and any
question of a disputed election to either House, shall be
determined by the House in which the question arises.

48. Until the Parliament otherwise provides, each Allowance to
members
senator and each member of the House of Representatives
shall receive an allowance of four hundred pounds a year,
to be reckoned from the day on which he takes his seat.

49. The powers, privileges, and immunities of the Privileges, etc.,
of Houses
Senate and of the House of Representatives, and of the
members and the committees of each House, shall be
such as are declared by the Parliament, and until declared
shall be those of the Commons House of Parliament of
the United Kingdom, and of its members and committees,
at the establishment of the Commonwealth.

50. Each House of the Parliament may make rules and Rules and
orders
orders with respect to—

(i) The mode in which its powers, privileges, and
immunities may be exercised and upheld:

(ii) The order and conduct of its business and proceedings either separately or jointly with the other House.

PART V
POWERS OF THE
PARLIAMENT

Legislative
powers of the
Parliament

PART V POWERS OF THE PARLIAMENT

51. The Parliament shall, subject to this Constitution, have power* to make laws for the peace, order, and good government of the Commonwealth with respect to:

(i) Trade and commerce with other countries, and among the States:

(ii) Taxation; but so as not to discriminate between States or parts of States:

(iii) Bounties on the production or export of goods, but so that such bounties shall be uniform throughout the Commonwealth:

(iv) Borrowing money on the public credit of the Commonwealth:

(v) Postal, telegraphic, telephonic, and other like services:

(vi) The naval and military defence of the Commonwealth and of the several States, and the control of the forces to execute and maintain the laws of the Commonwealth:

(vii) Lighthouses, lightships, beacons and buoys:

(viii) Astronomical and meteorological observations:

(ix) Quarantine:

(x) Fisheries in Australian waters beyond territorial limits.

(xi) Census and statistics:

(xii) Currency, coinage, and legal tender:

(xiii) Banking, other than State banking; also State banking extending beyond the limits of the State concerned, the incorporation of banks, and the issue of paper money:

(xiv) Insurance, other than State insurance; also

*The following Imperial Acts extended the legislative powers of the Parliament of the Commonwealth:

Whaling Industry (Regulation) Act 1934, section 15.
Geneva Convention Act 1937, section 2.
Emergency Powers (Defence) Act 1939, section 5.
Army and Air Force (Annual) Act, 1940, section 3.

[168]

State insurance extending beyond the limits of the State concerned:

(xv) Weights and measures:

(xvi) Bills of exchange and promissory notes:

(xvii) Bankruptcy and insolvency:

(xviii) Copyrights, patents of inventions and designs, and trade marks:

(xix) Naturalization and aliens:

(xx) Foreign corporations, and trading or financial corporations formed within the limits of the Commonwealth:

(xxi) Marriage:

(xxii) Divorce and matrimonial causes; and in relation thereto, parental rights, and the custody and guardianship of infants:

(xxiii) Invalid and old-age pensions:

(xxiiiA) The provision of maternity allowances, widows' pensions, child endowment, unemployment, pharmaceutical, sickness and hospital benefits, medical and dental services (but not so as to authorize any form of civil conscription), benefits to students and family allowances: *Inserted by No. 31, 1946, s. 2*

(xxiv) The service and execution throughout the Commonwealth of the civil and criminal process and the judgments of the courts of the States:

(xxv) The recognition throughout the Commonwealth of the laws, the public Acts and records, and the judicial proceedings of the States:

(xxvi) The people of any race, other than the aboriginal race in any State, for whom it is deemed necessary to make special laws:

(xxvii) Immigration and emigration:

(xxviii) The influx of criminals:

(xxix) External affairs:

(xxx) The relations of the Commonwealth with the islands of the Pacific:

(xxxi) The acquisition of property on just terms from any State or person for any purpose in respect of which the Parliament has power to make laws:

(xxxii) The control of railways with respect to transport for the naval and military purposes of the Commonwealth:

(xxxiii) The acquisition, with the consent of a State, of any railways of the State on terms arranged between the Commonwealth and the State:

(xxxiv) Railway construction and extension in any State with the consent of that State:

(xxxv) Conciliation and arbitration for the prevention and settlement of industrial disputes extending beyond the limits of any one State:

(xxxvi) Matters in respect of which this Constitution makes provision until the Parliament otherwise provides:

(xxxvii) Matters referred★ to the Parliament of the Commonwealth by the Parliament or Parliaments of any State or States, but so that the law shall extend only to States by whose Parliaments the matter is referred, or which afterwards adopt the law:

(xxxviii) The exercise within the Commonwealth, at the request or with the concurrence of the Parliaments of all the States, directly concerned, of any power which can at the establishment of this Constitution be exercised only by the Parliament of the United Kingdom or by the Federal Council of Australasia:

(xxxix) Matters incidental to the execution of any power vested by this Constitution in the Parliament or in either House thereof, or in the Government of the Commonwealth, or in the Federal Judicature, or in any department or other of the Commonwealth.

Exclusive powers of the Parliament

52. The Parliament shall, subject to this Constitution, have exclusive power to make laws for the peace, order, and good government of the Commonwealth with respect to—

(i) The seat of government of the Commonwealth,

★ For footnote see opposite page.

and all places acquired by the Commonwealth for
public purposes:
(ii) Matters relating to any department of the public
service the control of which is by this Constitution
transferred to the Executive Government of the
Commonwealth:
(iii) Other matters declared by this Constitution to be
within the exclusive power of the Parliament.

* The following Acts have been passed by the Parliaments of the States to refer
matters to the Parliament of the Commonwealth:

State	Number	Short Title	How Affected
New South Wales	No. 65, 1915	Commonwealth Powers (War) Act, 1915	Expired 9th January, 1921; *see* s. 5
	No. 33, 1942	Commonwealth Powers Act, 1942	Expired; *see* s. 4
	No. 18, 1943	Commonwealth Powers Act, 1943	Expired; *see* s. 4
	No. 40, 1949	Liquid Fuel Act, 1949	Expired 31st August, 1950
Victoria	No. 3108	Commonwealth Powers (Air Navigation) Act, 1920	Repealed by No. 4502
	No. 3658	Commonwealth Arrangements Act, 1928 (Part III)	Repealed by No. 4502
	No. 4009	Debt Conversion Agreement Act, 1931 (No. 2)	
	No. 4950	Commonwealth Powers Act, 1943	Not proclaimed to come into operation and cannot now be so proclaimed
Queensland	12 Geo. V. No. 30	The Commonwealth Powers (Air Navigation) Act of 1921	Repealed by 1 Geo. VI. No. 8
	22 Geo. V. No. 30	The Commonwealth Legislative Power Act, 1931	—
	7 Geo. VI. No. 19	Commonwealth Powers Act, 1943	Expired; *see* s. 4
	13 Geo. VI. No. 45	The Liquid Fuel Act of 1949	Expired 31st August, 1950
	14 Geo. VI. No. 2	The Commonwealth Powers (Air Transport) Act of 1950	—
South Australia	No. 1469, 1921	Commonwealth Powers (Navigation) Act, 1921	Repealed by No. 2352 of 1937
	No. 2061, 1931	Commonwealth Legislative Power Act, 1931	—
	No. 3, 1943	Commonwealth Powers Act, 1943	Expired; *see* s. 5
Western Australia	No. 4, 1943	Commonwealth Powers Act, 1943	Amended by No. 30, 1947; expired; *see* s. 4
	No. 57, 1945	Commonwealth Powers Act, 1945	Amended by Nos. 31, 73 and 81 of 1947; expired 31st December, 1948
	No. 30, 1947	Commonwealth Powers Act, 1943, Amendment Act, 1947	Expired; *see* No. 4, 1943
	No. 31, 1947	Commonwealth Powers Act, 1945, Amendment Act, 1947	Expired 31st December, 1948
	No. 73, 1947	Commonwealth Powers Act, 1945, Amendment Act (No. 2), 1947	Expired 31st December, 1948
	No. 81, 1947	Commonwealth Powers Act, 1945–1947, Amendment (Continuance) Act, 1947	Expired 31st December, 1948
	No. 21, 1949	Liquid Fuel (Emergency Provisions) Act, 1949	Expired 31st December, 1950
Tasmania	11 Geo. V. No. 42	Commonwealth Powers (Air Navigation) Act, 1920	Repealed by 1 Geo. VI. No. 14
	No. 46, 1952	Commonwealth Powers (Air Transport) Act, 1952	—

Powers of the
Houses in
respect of
legislation

53. Proposed laws appropriating revenue or moneys, or imposing taxation, shall not originate in the Senate. But a proposed law shall not be taken to appropriate revenue or moneys, or to impose taxation, by reason only of its containing provisions for the imposition or appropriation of fines or other pecuniary penalties, or for the demand or payment or appropriation of fees for licences, or fees for services under the proposed law.

The Senate may not amend proposed laws imposing taxation, or proposed laws appropriating revenue or moneys for the ordinary annual services of the Government.

The Senate may not amend any proposed law so as to increase any proposed charge or burden on the people.

The Senate may at any stage return to the House of Representatives any proposed law which the Senate may not amend, requesting, by message, the omission or amendment of any items or provisions therein. And the House of Representatives may, if it thinks fit, make any of such omissions or amendments, with or without modifications.

Except as provided in this section, the Senate shall have equal power with the House of Representatives in respect of all proposed laws.

Appropriation
Bills

54. The proposed law which appropriates revenue or moneys for the ordinary annual services of the Government shall deal only with such appropriation.

Tax Bill

55. Laws imposing taxation shall deal only with the imposition of taxation, and any provision therein dealing with any other matter shall be of no effect.

Laws imposing taxation, except laws imposing duties of customs or of excise, shall deal with one subject of taxation only; but laws imposing duties of customs shall deal with duties of customs only, and laws imposing duties of excise shall deal with duties of excise only.

Recommenda-
tion of money
votes

56. A vote, resolution, or proposed law for the appropriation of revenue or moneys shall not be passed unless the purpose of the appropriation has in the same session been recommended by message of the Governor-General to the House in which the proposal originated.

[172]

57. If the House of Representatives passes any pro- posed law, and the Senate rejects or fails to pass it or passes it with amendments to which the House of Representatives will not agree, and if after an interval of three months the House of Representatives, in the same or the next session, again passes the proposed law with or without any amendments which have been made, suggested, or agreed to by the Senate, and the Senate rejects or fails to pass it, or passes it with amendments to which the House of Representatives will not agree, the Governor-General may dissolve the Senate and the House of Representatives simultaneously. But such dissolution shall not take place within six months before the date of the expiry of the House of Representatives by effluxion of time.

If after such dissolution the House of Representatives again passes the proposed law, with or without any amendments which have been made, suggested, or agreed to by the Senate, and the Senate rejects or fails to pass it, or passes it with amendments to which the House of Representatives will not agree, the Governor-General may convene a joint sitting of the members of the Senate and of the House of Representatives.

The members present at the joint sitting may deliberate and shall vote together upon the proposed law as last proposed by the House of Representatives, and upon amendments, if any, which have been made therein by one House and not agreed to by the other, and any such amendments which are affirmed by an absolute majority of the total number of the members of the Senate and House of Representatives shall be taken to have been carried, and if the proposed law, with the amendments, if any, so carried is affirmed by an absolute majority of the total number of the members of the Senate and House of Representatives, it shall be taken to have been duly passed by both Houses of the Parliament, and shall be presented to the Governor-General for the Queen's assent.

58. When a proposed law passed by both Houses of the Parliament is presented to the Governor-General for the Queen's assent, he shall declare, according to his

discretion, but subject to this Constitution, that he assents in the Queen's name, or that he withholds assent, or that he reserves the law for the Queen's pleasure.

Recommendations by Governor-General

The Governor-General may return to the House in which it originated any proposed law so presented to him, and may transmit therewith any amendments which he may recommend, and the Houses may deal with the recommendation.

Disallowance by the Queen

59. The Queen may disallow any law within one year from the Governor-General's assent, and such disallowance on being made known by the Governor-General by speech or message to each of the Houses of the Parliament, or by Proclamation, shall annul the law from the day when the disallowance is so made known.

Signification of Queen's pleasure on Bills reserved

60. A proposed law reserved for the Queen's pleasure shall not have any force unless and until within two years from the day on which it was presented to the Governor-General for the Queen's assent the Governor-General makes known, by speech or message to each of the Houses of the Parliament, or by Proclamation, that it has received the Queen's assent.

Chapter II The Government

CHAPTER II

THE EXECUTIVE GOVERNMENT

Executive power

61. The executive power of the Commonwealth is vested in the Queen and is exerciseable by the Governor-General as the Queen's representative, and extends to the execution and maintenance of this Constitution, and of the laws of the Commonwealth.

Federal Executive Council

62. There shall be a Federal Executive Council to advise the Governor-General in the government of the Commonwealth, and the members of the Council shall be chosen and summoned by the Governor-General and sworn as Executive Councillors, and shall hold office during his pleasure.

Provisions referring to Governor-General

63. The provisions of this Constitution referring to the Governor-General in Council shall be construed as referring to the Governor-General acting with the advice of the Federal Executive Council.

64. The Governor-General may appoint officers to administer such departments of State of the Commonwealth as the Governor-General in Council may establish. **Minister of state**

Such officers shall hold office during the pleasure of the Governor-General. They shall be members of the Federal Executive Council, and shall be the Queen's Ministers of State for the Commonwealth. **Ministers to sit in Parliament**

After the first general election no Minister of State shall hold office for a longer period than three months unless he is or becomes a senator or a member of the House of Representatives.

65. Until the Parliament otherwise provides, the Ministers of State shall not exceed seven in number, and shall hold such offices as the Parliament prescribes, or, in the absence of provision, as the Governor-General directs. **Number of Ministers**

66. There shall be payable to the Queen out of the Consolidated Revenue Fund of the Commonwealth, for the salaries of the Ministers of State, an annual sum which, until the Parliament otherwise provides, shall not exceed twelve thousand pounds a year. **Salaries of Ministers**

67. Until the Parliament otherwise provides, the appointment and removal of all other officers of the Executive Government of the Commonwealth shall be vested in the Governor-General in Council, unless the appointment is delegated by the Governor-General in Council or by a law of the Commonwealth to some other authority. **Appointment of civil servants**

68. The command in chief of the naval and military forces of the Commonwealth is vested in the Governor-General as the Queen's representative. **Command of naval and military forces**

69. On a date or dates to be proclaimed by the Governor-General after the establishment of the Commonwealth the following departments of the public service in each State shall become transferred to the Commonwealth: **Transfer of certain departments**

Posts, telegraphs, and telephones
Naval and military defence:
Lighthouses, lightships, beacons, and buoys:
Quarantine.

But the departments of customs and of excise in each

State shall become transferred to the Commonwealth on its establishment.

70. In respect of matters which, under this Constitution, pass to the Executive Government of the Commonwealth, all powers and functions which at the establishment of the Commonwealth are vested in the Governor of a Colony, or in the Governor of a Colony with the advice of his Executive Council, or in any authority of a Colony, shall vest in the Governor-General, or in the Governor-General in Council, or in the authority exercising similar powers under the Commonwealth, as the case requires.

CHAPTER III

THE JUDICATURE

71. The judicial power of the Commonwealth shall be vested in a Federal Supreme Court, to be called the High Court of Australia, and in such other federal courts as the Parliament creates, and in such other courts as it invests with federal jurisdiction. The High Court shall consist of a Chief Justice, and so many other Justices, not less than two, as the Parliament prescribes.

72. The Justices of the High Court and of the other courts created by the Parliament

(i) Shall be appointed by the Governor-General in Council:

(ii) Shall not be removed except by the Governor-General in Council, on an address from both Houses of the Parliament in the same session, praying for such removal on the ground of proved misbehaviour or incapacity:

(iii) Shall receive such remuneration as the Parliament may fix; but the remuneration shall not be diminished during their continuance in office:

73. The High Court shall have jurisdiction, with such exceptions and subject to such regulations as the Parliament prescribes, to hear and determine appeals from all judgments, decrees, orders, and sentences:

[176]

(i) Of any Justice or Justices exercising the original jurisdiction of the High Court:

(ii) Of any other federal court, or court exercising federal jurisdiction; or of the Supreme Court of any State, or of any other court of any State from which at the establishment of the Commonwealth an appeal lies to the Queen in Council:

(iii) Of the Inter-State Commission, but as to questions of law only:

and the judgment of the High Court in all such cases shall be final and conclusive.

But no exception or regulation prescribed by the Parliament shall prevent the High Court from hearing and determining any appeal from the Supreme Court of a State in any matter in which at the establishment of the Commonwealth an appeal lies from such Supreme Court to the Queen in Council.

Until the Parliament otherwise provides, the conditions of and restrictions on appeals to the Queen in Council from the Supreme Courts of the several States shall be applicable to appeals from them to the High Court.

74. No appeal shall be permitted to the Queen in Council from a decision of the High Court upon any question, however arising, as to the limits inter se of the Constitutional powers of the Commonwealth and those of any State or States, or as to the limits inter se of the Constitutional powers of any two or more States, unless the High Court shall certify that the question is one which ought to be determined by Her Majesty in Council. *Appeal to Queen in Council*

The High Court may so certify if satisfied that for any special reason the certificate should be granted, and thereupon an appeal shall lie to Her Majesty in Council on the question without further leave.

Except as provided in this section, this Constitution shall not impair any right which the Queen may be pleased to exercise by virtue of Her Royal prerogative to grant special leave of appeal from the High Court to Her Majesty in Council. The Parliament may make laws limiting the matters in which such leave may be asked, but proposed laws containing any such limitation shall be reserved by the Governor-General for Her Majesty's pleasure.

Original jurisdiction of High Court

75. In all matters
   (i) Arising under any treaty:
   (ii) Affecting consuls or other representatives of other countries:
   (iii) In which the Commonwealth, or a person suing or being sued on behalf of the Commonwealth, is a party:
   (iv) Between States, or between residents of different States, or between a State and a resident of another State:
   (v) In which a writ of Mandamus or prohibition or an injunction is sought against an officer of the Commonwealth:

the High Court shall have original jurisdiction.

Additional original jurisdiction

76. The Parliament may make laws conferring original jurisdiction on the High Court in any matter
   (i) Arising under this Constitution, or involving its interpretation:
   (ii) Arising under any laws made by the Parliament:
   (iii) Of Admiralty and maritime jurisdiction:
   (iv) Relating to the same subject-matter claimed under the laws of different States.

Power to define jurisdiction

77. With respect to any of the matters mentioned in the last two sections the Parliament may make laws—
   (i) Defining the jurisdiction of any federal court other than the High Court:
   (ii) Defining the extent to which the jurisdiction of any federal court shall be exclusive of that which belongs to or is vested in the courts of the States:
   (iii) Investing any court of a State with federal jurisdiction.

Proceedings against Commonwealth or State

78. The Parliament may make laws conferring rights to proceed against the Commonwealth or a State in respect of matters within the limits of the judicial power.

Number of judges

79. The federal jurisdiction of any court may be exercised by such number of judges as the Parliament prescribes.

Trial by jury

80. The trial on indictment of any offence against any law of the Commonwealth shall be by jury, and every

such trial shall be held in the State where the offence was committed, and if the offence was not committed within any State the trial shall be held at such place or places as the Parliament prescribes.

CHAPTER IV

FINANCE AND TRADE

81. All revenues or moneys raised or received by the Executive Government of the Commonwealth shall form one Consolidated Revenue Fund, to be appropriated for the purposes of the Commonwealth in the manner and subject to the charges and liabilities imposed by this Constitution.

Consolidated Revenue Fund

82. The costs, charges, and expenses incident to the collection, management, and receipt of the Consolidated Revenue Fund shall form the first charge thereon; and the revenue of the Commonwealth shall in the first instance be applied to the payment of the expenditure of the Commonwealth.

Expenditure charged thereon

83. No money shall be drawn from the Treasury of the Commonwealth except under appropriation made by law.

Money to be appropriated by law

But until the expiration of one month after the first meeting of the Parliament the Governor-General in Council may draw from the Treasury and expend such moneys as may be necessary for the maintenance of any department transferred to the Commonwealth and for the holding of the first elections for the Parliament.

84. When any department of the public service of a State becomes transferred to the Commonwealth, all officers of the department shall become subject to the control of the Executive Government of the Commonwealth.

Transfer of officers

Any such officer who is not retained in the service of the Commonwealth shall, unless he is appointed to some other office of equal emolument in the public service of the State, be entitled to receive from the State any pension, gratuity, or other compensation, payable under the law of the State on the abolition of his office.

Any such officer who is retained in the service of the

Commonwealth shall preserve all his existing and accruing rights, and shall be entitled to retire from office at the time, and on the pension or retiring allowance, which would be permitted by the law of the State if his service with the Commonwealth were a continuation of his service with the State. Such pension or retiring allowance shall be paid to him by the Commonwealth; but the State shall pay to the Commonwealth a part thereof, to be calculated on the proportion which his term of service with the State bears to his whole term of service, and for the purpose of the calculation his salary shall be taken to be that paid to him by the State at the time of the transfer.

Any officer who is, at the establishment of the Commonwealth, in the public service of a State, and who is, by consent of the Governor of the State with the advice of the Executive Council thereof transferred to the public service of the Commonwealth, shall have the same rights as if he had been an officer of a department transferred to the Commonwealth and were retained in the service of the Commonwealth.

Transfer of property of State

85. When any department of the public service of a State is transferred to the Commonwealth—

(i) All property of the State of any kind, used exclusively in connexion with the department, shall become vested in the Commonwealth; but, in the case of the departments controlling customs and excise and bounties, for such time only as the Governor-General in Council may declare to be necessary:

(ii) The Commonwealth may acquire any property of the State, of any kind used, but not exclusively used in connexion with the department, the value thereof shall, if no agreement can be made, be ascertained in, as nearly as may be, the manner in which the value of land, or of an interest in land, taken by the State for public purposes is ascertained under the law of the State in force at the establishment of the Commonwealth:

(iii) The Commonwealth shall compensate the State for the value of any property passing to the Commonwealth under this section; if no agreement can be made as to the mode of compensation, it shall be determined under laws to be made by the Parliament:

(iv) The Commonwealth shall, at the date of the transfer, assume the current obligations of the State in respect of the department transferred.

86. On the establishment of the Commonwealth, the collection and control of duties of customs and of excise, and the control of the payment of bounties, shall pass to the Executive Government of the Commonwealth.

87. During a period of ten years after the establishment of the Commonwealth and thereafter until the Parliament otherwise provides, of the net revenue of the Commonwealth from duties of customs and of excise not more than one-fourth shall be applied annually by the Commonwealth towards its expenditure.

The balance shall, in accordance with this Constitution, be paid to the several States, or applied towards the payment of interest on debts of the several States taken over by the Commonwealth.

88. Uniform duties of customs shall be imposed within two years after the establishment of the Commonwealth. *Uniform duties of customs*

89. Until the imposition of uniform duties of customs *Payment to States before uniform duties*

(i) The Commonwealth shall credit to each State the revenues collected therein by the Commonwealth.

(ii) The Commonwealth shall debit to each State—

(*a*) The expenditure therein of the Commonwealth incurred solely for the maintenance or continuance, as at the time of transfer, of any department transferred from the State to the Commonwealth;

(*b*) The proportion of the State, according to the number of its people, in the other expenditure of the Commonwealth.

(iii) The Commonwealth shall pay to each State month by month the balance (if any) in favour of the State.

90. On the imposition of uniform duties of customs the power of the Parliament to impose duties of customs and of excise, and to grant bounties on the production or export of goods, shall become exclusive. *Exclusive power over customs, excise, and bounties*

[181]

AUSTRALIAN COMMONWEALTH

On the imposition of uniform duties of customs all laws of the several States imposing duties of customs or of excise, or offering bounties on the production or export of goods, shall cease to have effect, but any grant of or agreement for any such bounty lawfully made by or under the authority of the Government of any State shall be taken to be good if made before the thirtieth day of June, one thousand eight hundred and ninety-eight, and not otherwise.

Exceptions as to bounties

91. Nothing in this Constitution prohibits a State from granting any aid to or bounty on mining for gold, silver, or other metals, nor from granting, with the consent of both Houses of the Parliament of the Commonwealth expressed by resolution, any aid to or bounty on the production or export of goods.

Trade within the Commonwealth to be free

92. On the imposition of uniform duties of customs, trade, commerce, and intercourse among the States, whether by means of internal carriage or ocean navigation, shall be absolutely free.

But notwithstanding anything in this Constitution, goods imported before the imposition of uniform duties of customs into any State, or into any colony which, whilst the goods remain therein, becomes a State, shall, on thence passing into another State within two years after the imposition of such duties, be liable to any duty chargeable on the importation of such goods into the Commonwealth, less any duty paid in respect of the goods on their importation.

Payment to States for five years after uniform Tariffs

93. During the first five years after the imposition of uniform duties of customs, and thereafter until the Parliament otherwise provides—

(i) The duties of customs chargeable on goods imported into a State and afterwards passing into another State for consumption, and the duties of excise paid on goods produced or manufactured in a State and afterwards passing into another State for consumption, shall be taken to have been collected not in the former but in the latter State:

(ii) Subject to the last sub-section, the Commonwealth shall credit revenue, debit expenditure, and pay balances to the several States as prescribed for the period preceding the imposition of uniform duties of customs.

94. After five years from the imposition of uniform duties of customs, the Parliament may provide, on such basis as it deems fair, for the monthly payment to the several States of all surplus revenue of the Commonwealth.

Distribution of surplus

95. Notwithstanding anything in this Constitution, the Parliament of the State of Western Australia, if that State be an Original State, may, during the first five years after the imposition of uniform duties of customs, impose duties of customs on goods passing into that State and not originally imported from beyond the limits of the Commonwealth; and such duties shall be collected by the Commonwealth.

Customs duties of Western Australia

But any duty so imposed on any goods shall not exceed during the first of such years the duty chargeable on the goods under the law of Western Australia in force at the imposition of uniform duties, and shall not exceed during the second, third, fourth, and fifth of such years respectively, four-fifths, three-fifths, two-fifths, and one-fifth of such latter duty, and all duties imposed under this section shall cease at the expiration of the fifth year after the imposition of uniform duties.

If at any time during the five years the duty on any goods under this section is higher than the duty imposed by the Commonwealth on the importation of the like goods, then such higher duty shall be collected on the goods when imported into Western Australia from beyond the limits of the Commonwealth.

96. During a period of ten years after the establishment of the Commonwealth and thereafter until the Parliament otherwise provides, the Parliament may grant financial assistance to any State on such terms and conditions as the Parliament thinks fit.

Financial assistance to States

97. Until the Parliament otherwise provides, the laws in force in any Colony which has become or becomes a State with respect to the receipt of revenue and the expenditure of money on account of the Government of the Colony, and the review and audit of such receipt and expenditure, shall apply to the receipt of revenue and

Audit

N

the expenditure of money on account of the Commonwealth in the State in the same manner as if the Commonwealth, or the Government or an officer of the Commonwealth, were mentioned whenever the Colony, or the Government or an officer of the Colony, is mentioned.

Trade and commerce includes navigation and State railways

98. The power of the Parliament to make laws with respect to trade and commerce extends to navigation and shipping, and to railways the property of any State.

Commonwealth not to give preference

99. The Commonwealth shall not, by any law or regulation of trade, commerce, or revenue, give preference to one State or any part thereof over another State or any part thereof.

Nor abridge right to use water

100. The Commonwealth shall not, by any law or regulation of trade or commerce, abridge the right of a State or of the residents therein to the reasonable use of the waters of rivers for conservation or irrigation.

Inter-State Commission

101. There shall be an Inter-State Commission, with such powers of adjudication and administration as the Parliament deems necessary for the execution and maintenance, within the Commonwealth, of the provisions of this Constitution relating to trade and commerce, and of all laws made thereunder.

Parliament may forbid preferences by State

102. The Parliament may by any law with respect to trade or commerce forbid, as to railways, any preference or discrimination by any State, or by any authority constituted under a State, if such preference or discrimination is undue and unreasonable, or unjust to any State; due regard being had to the financial responsibilities incurred by any State in connexion with the construction and maintenance of its railways. But no preference or discrimination shall, within the meaning of this section, be taken to be undue and unreasonable, or unjust to any State, unless so adjudged by the Inter-State Commission.

Commissioners' appointment, tenure, and remuneration

103. The members of the Inter-State Commission—

(i) Shall be appointed by the Governor-General in Council:

(ii) Shall hold office for seven years, but may be removed within that time by the Governor-General in Council, on an address from both Houses of the Parliament in the same session praying for such removal on the ground of proved misbehaviour or incapacity:

(iii) Shall receive such remuneration as the Parliament may fix; but such remuneration shall not be diminished during their continuance in office.

104. Nothing in this Constitution shall render unlawful any rate for the carriage of goods upon a railway, the property of a State, if the rate is deemed by the Inter-State Commission to be necessary for the development of the territory of the State, and if the rate applies equally to goods within the State and to goods passing into the State from other States.

Saving of certain rates

105. The Parliament may take over from the States their public debts or a proportion thereof according to the respective numbers of their people as shown by the latest statistics of the Commonwealth, and may convert, renew, or consolidate such debts, or any part thereof; and the States shall indemnify the Commonwealth in respect of the debts taken over, and thereafter the interest payable in respect of the debts shall be deducted and retained from the portions of the surplus revenue of the Commonwealth payable to the several States, or if such surplus is insufficient, or if there is no surplus, then the deficiency or the whole amount shall be paid by the several States.

Taking over public debts of States.
Altered by No. 3, 1910, s. 2

105A.—(1) The Commonwealth may make agreements with the States with respect to the public debts of the States, including—

Agreements with respect to State debts.
Inserted by No. 1, 1929, s. 2

(a) the taking over of such debts by the Commonwealth;

(b) the management of such debts;

(c) the payment of interest and the provision and management of sinking funds in respect of such debts;

(d) the consolidation, renewal, conversion, and redemption of such debts;

(e) the indemnification of the Commonwealth by the States in respect of debts taken over by the Commonwealth; and

(f) the borrowing of money by the States or by the Commonwealth, or by the Commonwealth for the States.

(2) The Parliament may make laws for validating any such agreement made before the commencement of this section.

(3) The Parliament may make laws for the carrying out by the parties thereto of any such agreement.

(4) Any such agreement may be varied or rescinded by the parties thereto.

(5) Every such agreement and any such variation thereof shall be binding upon the Commonwealth and the States parties thereto nothwithstanding anything contained in this Constitution or the Constitution of the several States or in any law of the Parliament of the Commonwealth or of any State.

(6) The powers conferred by this section shall not be construed as being limited in any way by the provisions of section one hundred and five of this Constitution.

CHAPTER V
THE STATES

CHAPTER V

THE STATES

Saving of
Constitutions

106. The Constitution of each State of the Commonwealth shall, subject to this Constitution, continue as at the establishment of the Commonwealth, or as at the admission or establishment of the State, as the case may be, until altered in accordance with the Constitution of the State.

Saving of power
of State
Parliaments

107. Every power of the Parliament of a Colony which has become or becomes a State, shall, unless it is by this Constitution exclusively vested in the Parliament of the Commonwealth or withdrawn from the Parliament of the State, continue as at the establishment of the Commonwealth, or as at the admission or establishment of the State, as the case may be.

Saving of State
laws

108. Every law in force in a Colony which has become or becomes a State, and relating to any matter within the powers of the Parliament of the Commonwealth, shall, subject to this Constitution, continue in force in the State: and, until provision is made in that behalf by the Parliament of the Commonwealth, the Parliament of the State shall have such powers of alteration and of repeal

in respect of any such law as the Parliament of the Colony had until the Colony became a State.

109. When a law of a State is inconsistent with a law of the Commonwealth, the latter shall prevail, and the former shall, to the extent of the inconsistency, be invalid.

Inconsistency of laws

110. The provisions of this Constitution relating to the Governor of a State extend and apply to the Governor for the time being of the State, or other chief executive officer or administrator of the government of the State.

Provisions referring to Governor

111. The Parliament of a State may surrender any part of the State to the Commonwealth; and upon such surrender, and the acceptance thereof by the Commonwealth, such part of the State shall become subject to the exclusive jurisdiction of the Commonwealth.

States may surrender territory

112. After uniform duties of customs have been imposed, a State may levy on imports or exports, or on goods passing into or out of the State, such charges as may be necessary for executing the inspection laws of the State; but the net produce of all charges so levied shall be for the use of the Commonwealth; and any such inspection laws may be annulled by the Parliament of the Commonwealth.

States may levy charges for inspection laws

113. All fermented, distilled, or other intoxicating liquids passing into any State or remaining therein for use, consumption, sale, or storage, shall be subject to the laws of the State as if such liquids had been produced in the State.

Intoxicating liquids

114. A State shall not, without the consent of the Parliament of the Commonwealth, raise or maintain any naval or military force, or impose any tax on property of any kind belonging to the Commonwealth, nor shall the Commonwealth impose any tax on property of any kind belonging to a State.

States may not raise forces. Taxation of property of Commonwealth or State

115. A State shall not coin money, nor make anything but gold and silver coin a legal tender in payment of debts.

States not to coin money

116. The Commonwealth shall not make any law for establishing any religion, or for imposing any religious observance, or for prohibiting the free exercise of any religion, and no religious test shall be required as a qualification for any office or public trust under the Commonwealth.

Commonwealth not to legislate in respect of religion

117. A subject of the Queen, resident in any State, shall not be subject in any other State to any disability or discrimination which would not be equally applicable to him if he were a subject of the Queen resident in such other State.

118. Full faith and credit shall be given, throughout the Commonwealth, to the laws, the public Acts and records, and the judicial proceedings of every State.

119. The Commonwealth shall protect every State against invasion and, on the application of the Executive Government of the State, against domestic violence.

120. Every State shall make provision for the detention in its prisons of persons accused or convicted of offences against the laws of the Commonwealth, and for the punishment of persons convicted of such offences, and the Parliament of the Commonwealth may make laws to give effect to this provision.

CHAPTER VI

NEW STATES

121. The Parliament may admit to the Commonwealth or establish new States, and may upon such admission or establishment make or impose such terms and conditions, including the extent of representation in either House of the Parliament, as it thinks fit.

122. The Parliament may make laws for the government of any territory surrendered by any State to and accepted by the Commonwealth, or of any Territory placed by the Queen under the authority of and accepted by the Commonwealth, or otherwise acquired by the Commonwealth, and may allow the representation of such territory in either House of the Parliament to the extent and on the terms which it thinks fit.

123. The Parliament of the Commonwealth may, with the consent of the Parliament of a State, and the approval of the majority of the electors of the State voting upon the question, increase, diminish, or otherwise alter the limits of the State, upon such terms and conditions as may be agreed on, and may, with the like consent, make provision respecting the effect and operation of any

increase or diminution or alteration of territory in relation to any State affected.

124. A new State may be formed by separation of territory from a State, but only with the consent of the Parliament thereof, and a new State may be formed by the union of two or more States or parts of States, but only with the consent of the Parliaments of the States affected.

Formation of new States

CHAPTER VII
MISCELLANEOUS

CHAPTER VII
MISCELLANEOUS

125. The seat of Government of the Commonwealth shall be determined by the Parliament, and shall be within territory which shall have been granted to or acquired by the Commonwealth, and shall be vested in and belong to the Commonwealth, and shall be in the State of New South Wales, and be distant not less than one hundred miles from Sydney.

Seat of Government

Such territory shall contain an area of not less than one hundred square miles, and such portion thereof as shall consist of Crown lands shall be granted to the Commonwealth without any payment therefor.

The Parliament shall sit at Melbourne until it meet at the seat of Government.

126. The Queen may authorize the Governor-General to appoint any person, or any persons jointly or severally, to be his deputy or deputies within any part of the Commonwealth, and in that capacity to exercise during the pleasure of the Governor-General such powers and functions of the Governor-General as he thinks fit to assign to such deputy or deputies, subject to any limitations expressed or directions given by the Queen; but the appointment of such deputy or deputies shall not affect the exercise by the Governor-General himself of any power or function.

Power to Her Majesty to authorize Governor-General to appoint deputies

127. In reckoning the numbers of the people of the Commonwealth, or of a State or other part of the Commonwealth, aboriginal natives shall not be counted.

Aborigines not to be counted in reckoning population

CHAPTER VIII

ALTERATION OF THE CONSTITUTION

Mode of
altering the
Constitution

128. This Constitution shall not be altered except in the following manner:

The proposed law for the alteration thereof must be passed by an absolute majority of each House of the Parliament, and not less than two nor more than six months after its passage through both Houses the proposed law shall be submitted in each State to the electors qualified to vote for the election of members of the House of Representatives.

But if either House passes any such proposed law by an absolute majority, and the other House rejects or fails to pass it or passes it with any amendment to which the first-mentioned House will not agree, and if after an interval of three months the first-mentioned House in the same or the next session again passes the proposed law by an absolute majority with or without any amendment which has been made or agreed to by the other House, and such other House rejects or fails to pass it or passes it with any amendment to which the first-mentioned House will not agree, the Governor-General may submit the proposed law as last proposed by the first-mentioned House, and either with or without any amendments subsequently agreed to by both Houses, to the electors in each State qualified to vote for the election of the House of Representatives.

When a proposed law is submitted to the electors the vote shall be taken in such manner as the Parliament prescribes. But until the qualification of electors of members of the House of Representatives becomes uniform throughout the Commonwealth, only one-half the electors voting for and against the proposed law shall be counted in any State in which adult suffrage prevails.

And if in a majority of the States a majority of the electors voting approve the proposed law, and if a majority of all the electors voting also approve the proposed law, it shall be presented to the Governor-General for the Queen's assent.

No alteration diminishing the proportionate representation of any State in either House of the Parliament, or the minimum number of representatives of a State in the House of Representatives, or increasing, diminishing, or otherwise altering the limits of the State, or in any manner affecting the provisions of the Constitution in relation thereto, shall become law unless the majority of the electors voting in that State approve the proposed law.

SCHEDULE

Section 42.

OATH

I, *A.B.*, do swear that I will be faithful and bear true allegiance to Her Majesty Queen Victoria, Her heirs and successors according to law. So HELP ME GOD!

AFFIRMATION

I, *A.B.*, do solemnly and sincerely affirm and declare that I will be faithful and bear true allegiance to Her Majesty Queen Victoria, Her heirs and successors according to law.

(NOTE.—*The name of the King or Queen of the United Kingdom of Great Britain and Ireland for the time being is to be substituted from time to time.*)

Index

1. Principal references are in bold type, *e.g.* **5–25**
2. Legal cases quoted are arranged alphabetically under 'Cases cited'.
3. The *Appendix*, which consists of the full text of The Commonwealth of Australia Constitution Act, is *not* here indexed; but its headings and sub-headings will be found in its margins, while its chapter headings are on page 156.
4. '*bis*', '*ter*' or '*quat*' after a page reference means that the topic is dealt with two, three or four times *in separate paragraphs* on the page indicated; '*passim*' means 'here and there' (scattered references).